About The Author

Mark Waller is a professional artist, living and working in Lennox Head, on the North Coast of NSW, Australia. This is his first book, but it probably won't be his last.

Copyright © 2022 Mark Waller
All rights reserved. This book or any portion thereof
may not be reproduced or used in any manner whatsoever
without the express written permission of the publisher
except for the use of brief quotations in a book review.

Cover design Copyright © 2017 by Frankie Sharman
Book design and production by Frankie Sharman & Mark Waller
Typeset in Uniform, Times New Roman, Courier.

Printed in Australia

First Printing, 2022
ISBN: 978-0-6484507-1-9

Tangent Projects
2 Meaney Place
LENNOX HEAD NSW 2478

www.explore-acrylic-painting.com
www.markwaller.com.au

ExploreAcrylics

ExploreAcrylicPainting
MarkWallerArtist

@explore.acrylic.painting
@markwallerpaints

A catalogue record for this
book is available from the
National Library of Australia

IT'S ALL ABOUT

THE LIGHT

AN EXPERIENCE
Mark Waller

Acknowledgment of Country

I would like to acknowledge the traditional custodians of the land where these events and the making of this book took place. The Wahjuk people of the Walyalup Nation and the Nyangbul, Widjabul Wia-bal and Arakwal people of the Bundjalung Nation.

I'd like to acknowledge the Elders past, present and future, of a culture that has lived with the land for over 60,000 years, and whose wisdom I am just beginning to understand.

The experiences I've written about in this book have led me to have a deeper appreciation and respect for a culture with such a strong spiritual connection, and a deeper and more profound appreciation for our planet.

I'm in awe.

- *Mark Waller*

*Dedicated to my Dad.
I know he was proud of me.*

Introduction - 2020

I am not a writer. Occasionally, I thought I might write something, one day. It wasn't ever going to be this, and it certainly wasn't going to be about this. This, whatever 'this' is, has been, in a way, forced on me - but it is not in any way a burden. 'Gifted' to me is probably a better choice of words. I have loved writing it, and have even watched in awe as words rushed out of me in an effortless torrent. I'm happy to talk to anyone, about anything, at any time, yet writing always felt clumsy. Writing this wasn't like that for me - but I'll let you be the judge.

I've always considered there was something more to this world. Something beyond our ability to see easily. Perhaps energy, some form of divine force (or something). But I never felt that I should, or would, write a book about experiencing it. If I'm honest, I'm pretty sure that the vague idea of actually putting pen to paper about anything, was something that would've wafted off into the ether. Another one of those things I was going to do 'one day'.

The events of 2016 kicked me sideways in such a way that I can't stop writing this. I'm compelled to in a way I wouldn't have believed possible. I have to. I feel as though I've been told to by something much, MUCH bigger than me.

That statement needs some clarification before you read any further. There are aspects of this book that some people will not believe. There will be many aspects that can't be explained by 'rational' thinking. I completely understand as I would have been in the same place before my surgery. This is not something I would have written before that. There are concepts here that are probably outside the everyday experience for most people.

So thinking rationally; at the time of the experiences around the surgery, I was full of steroids, and a cocktail of drugs that probably only the neurosurgeons and pharmacists understand, including anaesthetics and pain blockers. And, I was in the highly emotional position of facing the possible end of my days, and all the conversations and imaginings that come with facing that reality.

To be clear, I'm not asking anyone to believe. In fact, I still find it hard to believe myself. In a nutshell, I had three specific experiences, each one with a different 'flavour'. The words I'm using here are indescribably inadequate, however, the best way I could find to touch on them is this:

The first experience was an introduction to what's behind everything. But it is incredibly difficult to understand, and articulate.

The second was an insight into how every thing (and every no-thing) is constructed. It's a difficult concept to comprehend. It can only be experienced.

The third was a way to communicate a sense of these experiences within our human framework and understanding. This may make more sense later on. Or not. We'll see.

All three of these experiences I have struggled to articulate within the limitations of language, and our 3D human framework. All my efforts to do this are my best, but still paltry and hollow compared to the rapturous reality.

I do hope though that in this story there will be gems that may give some insights into an altered way of living. It certainly has been a very cathartic experience getting it out of my head onto paper, and is something I read again and again. I'm hoping that by sharing this experience, it may prompt a shift in consciousness for those who are seeking that. Or alternatively, inspire others to find their own way to a similar place.

At the time of writing, the melanoma tumours in my lungs are classed as 'inert', and my brain is clear. Recent history suggests that I once would have had a 75% chance of developing another tumour in my brain. I mention this because, despite the cancer diagnosis and the possible outcomes from it, the events around my brain surgery have created a space in which I have managed to live with extraordinary bliss, patience and joy.

This story has changed me profoundly. I am gentler. I am much more present and calm. I laugh a lot, and, to a large degree, am content to just be. To be honest, it's driving my wife a little crazy. If I'm asked what I'd like to do, my answer is, 'I don't mind'. I tend to feel content wherever I am, which can be a tad annoying when people want a decision.

Despite the current positive outcomes, I am still prepared to die. I would, however, quite like to stay alive, and I feel that maintaining this state of peace around my cancer will be a big part of me outliving it, and enjoying a healthy long life.

Alive - 2017

The board is alive under my feet, humming with the water flying past it. It twitches, waiting for me to again tell it what to do. We have an agreement, the board and I. I tell it where to go and it trusts. That trust is often misplaced. For the final time on this glorious collaboration of water, weather and reef, the last wave of the session, I lean. The board changes direction and the North Pacific throws me across its crystalline face. I watch the coral fly past and under my fins, then feel them bite as I push them deep into the water and pick a line beyond the explosion of white water. I'm in the clear, on the shoulder, then paddling. I relax, the wave behind is smaller, the gentle cousin of the one I have just ridden.

I have cancer.

My shoulders are burning as I head for the boat, spent. The effort of getting my tired body into the boat has me collapsed on the hot deck, smiling, exhilarated, relieved. The boat bounces and the air is full of wind and the sounds of my surfing friends, reliving our glories and beatings. The warm wind takes the salty water from my skin and roughs my hair, leaving a thin crust to remind me.

The beach is beautiful. A picture postcard. The sand is fine, sticky and cool. The coconut juice runs down my arms and chin, down my throat, past the entrance to my lungs, past the place where the tumours lie. I thank the tumours for what they have taught me and firmly, but gently, tell them to leave.

I go back to the moment, back to the sand, the coconut and the colours of the tropics that hurl themselves at my senses. This is my life now. Moment, then moment, then moment. Each one glorious and magnificent. Occasionally the cancer appears in my thoughts, not ominous, just there. It arrives just in time to remind me of the preciousness of the moments in between. Curiously the awareness of the cancer is no less precious. It too is an experience to be savoured. There is a choice there, if it can be seen. Live with or without the cancer, or, suffer with the possibilities of it, and give up my joy of being alive. Mostly I choose the first option.

The coconut juice tickles and trickles slowly down my sore arms and salty skin, while the wind runs its warm fingers through my hair.

The Abyss - 2001

In the depths of the universe, the cosmic soup pulses. Energy moves across billions of light-years and matter is thrown across the darkness between stars. There is silence.

A tiny sound, so fragile and delicate, that it pierces, warms and softens even the endless abyss. A baby stirs, and a parent, barely asleep, slightly exasperated, sighs. There is another sound, voice, and a pause. That other voice croaks softly.

"I'll go."

A soft shaft of light cuts the cosmic soup, hinting at the floor of a room. The left foot lands, is met by the right, and the feet pad off toward the only sound in the dark; the child. Deep in the abyss, the father holds her. The light of the creation of everything falls softly on them, shaping their dance, drawing their embrace in barely seen lines across shoulders, faces and cheeks.

The sound of his hand padding flatly, gently on his child's backside, mimicking the pulse of her mother's heart when her body encased the child. He subconsciously recreates the ultimate safety of her womb, swaying gently, feeling his way back into his child's sleep and eventually, maybe his own. He sings, softly. 'Try not to get worried, try not to hold on to, problems that upset you, don't you know everything's alright, yes, everything's fine, and I want you to sleep well tonight.' The song from Jesus Christ Superstar emerges from his own memories and subtly becomes part of hers.

The baby settles slowly and gurgles. They dance on into the dark. He stays too long, savouring his child's warmth, tasting the love he is giving her. He can feel the smile in his chest, just another second... Eventually, he can take his hand from the child now asleep in the cot. The tiny frame leaves a numb spot in his forearm and left knee. His own bed pulses across the abyss, calling him. His feet return along the shaft of light on the floor, swirling dust and cosmic embers as they pass.

Sunlight

"What time?" his wife asks.

The man, still resisting consciousness, makes a sound that in no way gives a measurement, yet somehow tells all that needs to be told.

"I have no clue how you can rock her for so long," she wonders. "How do you do that?"

There is a pause and a groan. This one though is not an answer. Eventually, a vague sound emerges, and semi-formed words fall from the corner of his mouth into the folds of the blanket and out into the sunlight.

"I dunno. It somehow feels important. Like building something. A memory maybe?"

Some Years Later - 2007

The stars subside. The abyss slides away as the earth spins. The sunlight filters through the curtains.

The transition from asleep to awake is abrupt, cut by children giggling.

"On, off, on, off, on. Come on dad, WAKE UP!"

His eyelids, futile barriers to protect his efforts to remain unconscious, are pulled and pushed by tiny fingers begging for attention. Not conscious enough to be annoyed, he forces a laboured sound into the world.

"What's the time?"

A child's fingers find his eyes again, on, off, on, off.

Some Years Later, Again - 2011

Again the cosmic soup roils, penetrated only by the gentle sounds of sleep. The black softens; the early light begins to give the room its form. Morning creeps in further, and the stars recede into the wardrobes and corners.

The lump under the blanket stirs. The sounds he makes as he wakes are lost to the sound of children moving through the house; of domestic life. These noises sing love to him more than any other thing his family could do at that moment.

Family is what he wanted since he could remember. He loved being a father, a husband. It wasn't easy though. Bringing up children was challenging, but he tried to keep a balance between providing and being present. He made sure he'd been there for his girls' first steps and their first words. He was aware just how blessed he was, that many parents were not able to mould their lives to be there for those milestones. He knew how valuable these moments were, the preciousness of the lives he was constructing. The greatest gift he felt he could give his kids was a stable, loving, connected family; sometimes failing, but always trying.

Time fell through the gaps in living, taking some of the shine of family life with it. The fights about money were the worst. They seemed to say he was somehow failing them, that he was letting them down. They hurt. He was confused; he thought he was doing the right thing.

For him, money was not so important, just a means to an end. He didn't care too much what others thought about him. He was definitely not going to buy into the treadmill for 'acceptance'. To him, there was little motivation for that position. He was walking a line between his ideas about looking after the planet, about being there for his family, and yet resisting the push from the 'real' world to buy more, to have more, and to be more, by having more. He thought he had managed all of that reasonably well, though the pressure was still there, gnawing away in the background.

There were still voices of some who were close. They wanted more, something else. They couldn't see the world he saw or the way he saw it. His world was simple. There was magic in the tiniest things. Beetles, birds, water. It was difficult for him to see too much attraction in a car or shiny stuff. He wanted to stand in the rain with his kids, surf, and lie with them reading quietly on a Sunday afternoon.

These were the things that warmed him, and he was happy to do more of them, and have less stuff. He had found a balance of sorts. Sometimes slipping into one side more than the other, and then handling the consequences. He walked that rope, mostly enjoying the game, one foot in front of the other.

Headaches - 2015

The headaches were different. They were pre-announced by a strange kaleidoscopic halo effect, pretty shards of colour, flashing in the centre of his vision. They radiated outwards, almost making work impossible, and soon after were followed by nausea, which often forced him to lie somewhere quietly.

Maybe it was a blood sugar thing. The headache that followed the sparkles was horrible, but nowhere near as bad as some he'd experienced growing up. He hadn't had a migraine for a good few years, becoming used to their absence. These were becoming more regular though, and the threat of them had him keep a box of strong painkillers close.

He had experienced occasional bad headaches for as long as he could remember. When he was small he remembered them as horrific. They usually began as a small lump of greyish gravel behind his left eye. They pulsed and grew incrementally with each pump of his heart, expanding very gradually so he could see what was coming. Although knowing was no good thing.

The dread of the inevitable misery was almost as sharp as the discomfort of it. The headache would eventually become a boulder inside a cavity, which was dry, his brain rasping against the rough sharp bone of the insides of his skull. They eventually reduced him to a silent, darkened form in a silent darkened room, alone. Alone with a pulsing that was almost hallucinatory. The dry stone, rough and throbbing behind his eye, was almost seen, tasted. Everything hurt.

There was a period, from somewhere in his late thirties, when they mostly disappeared, leaving an easier void; a space where the concern of having a migraine used to live. There was a quietly celebrated lightness that lay over his relatively relaxed life. The odd headache wasn't a big deal. He had an idyllic lifestyle doing something he loved. He painted on canvas - big, wonderful, bright images of the area he lived in and loved. There was the added bonus of travelling to teach others these skills.

He could bend his work around the surf, taking advantage of conditions and the ability to avoid too many of the surfers who were moving to his small town. He lived to live, having made the decision early to make a life around lifestyle rather than money. He was happy with that choice. Having dodged that bullet, quite deliberately, he was quietly proud of himself for having done it, but also grateful for having the courage and ability to do it.

He'd been 'that' kid, the one who continually asked: why? Some slick suit telling him he needed to upgrade his car, home and clothes set off alarm bells. Why? To buy into this idea, he'd have to give up his lifestyle. For what?

These questions he repeated over and over, sometimes wearing out the patience of people in his circle. He couldn't see how having more 'things' made him a better person, and in the back of his mind there were always the questions… 'What would eventually happen to what he bought?' and 'What damage was done to the planet to make and use it?'

There was always a struggle with the reality that he needed to dip his toes into that world to survive it, but he'd found an equilibrium he could live with. Minimal harm on the world, and others, and survival for his family while having maximum fun with them. As well as lots of surfing, sitting under trees and feeling the planet hum. Just being.

Life was good.

Aside from the normal dramas associated with small children, an uncertain income stream, and a mortgage, he was happy. He worked from home and had been there after school, playing on the trampoline, laughing till he cried. Crazy, silly, fun children's games that brought them to their knees. He tended wounds and hugged - wonderful, sticky, fingers in the eyes, kid hugs. He considered those moments some of the greatest in his life. In those moments and others, he had unwittingly brushed against 'God'.

His babies were bigger now. Young women. He couldn't see it, but recently he'd been changing. He'd always been a bit of a hothead and, if he was honest, liked to be liked, despite often pretending not to care what others thought. He often tried just a little bit too hard to impress, exaggerating stories to entertain, but also to make himself appear a little bigger, a little… more.

This strategy didn't work all the time, and he was left feeling slightly hollow after his efforts. Occasionally he would resort to physicality. He wasn't small and was reasonably good at handling himself. He wasn't keen to go down the aggro path but sometimes found himself there anyway. He was, for the most part, an oversized Labrador puppy.

As his behaviour changed, the distance between him and his beloved girls grew. The space between them was widening, and the pain grew greater with the distance. He gradually lost his ability to manage this. He had always been able to find a way to his family, of somehow negotiating through whatever was going on; a way of easing them out of their problems or cleaning up his behaviour. But now… their souls were being torn apart. This was not the path he wanted.

Yet despite this, the money came in, and his business grew.

The Grey - 2016

Things were closing in. His world was becoming crowded. It was as though large, dull, grey, partially filled balloons crowded into his periphery, making it hard to see his world in its entirety. He had to work hard to focus on anything. Interactions, work, the simplest of tasks, were continually being obscured by the greyness.

He became frustrated easily. Overwhelmed and confused, the anger from his frustration spilled out far too quickly. He'd always expressed opinions about the injustices of the world at large and often been passionate about expressing them. Passionate but contained. Now, the news weighed him down. He'd had some hope before, but each new conflict, environmental crime and act of greed and mindlessness sat on his head and shoulders like sticky, grey, cloistering turds.

There were events where this frustration almost became physical, but his understanding of the events was obscured; complicated and yet flattened somehow. He struggled to find his way through it. Attempts were made to clean up his behaviour after he lost his cool, but these attempts were often stifled and thwarted by the 'grey weight'.

It seemed he was spiralling into a world of frustration and confusion that imposed more and more, preventing him from negotiating everyday life.

Everyone and everything was moving out of reach. He spent time alone, suffering from this distance, weeping for the gradual loss of his family life. The thing that meant the most.

The Split

"I want to make sure you girls can stay with me whenever you want. You can have a room each at your mum's, and a room each here."

His words were meant to be consoling; but their hollowness bounced off the empty walls, rebounding again and again. That hollowness was emphasised, the pain felt with every reverberation.

The question came.

'What am I doing? I don't want this.'

The thought was immediately justified internally and pushed into the corner as he looked around the new house, and at the list of things to be done.

The Trip

The exhibition in Perth had been planned for a long time. Some space and time away might be good for him. Perhaps the trip would be fun, good for business and just good in general. Some space just for him might help; a buffer to help him back on track.

Things weren't good now. How was he at this place? Why did everything seem completely overwhelming? There was an ominous feeling that had crept in, disrupted time and narrowed the world.

He moved at a frenetic pace, somehow thinking that activity would help. He kept moving relentlessly, almost to avoid stopping and looking at what was happening to his life.

For the most part he felt that he managed the work/life balance thing quite well, but now he worked long hours and was away a lot. It felt like running through treacle. All the effort brought him closer to his work goals, but stuff at home was shitty. He'd even been arguing badly with his precious girls.

"What is going on? Why can't I find my way through this?"

This was something new, and horrible. He'd been able to work through crappy emotional stuff before, but now, he didn't seem to be able to separate himself, to look at his life from a distance to gain some clarity. He was lost.

Blues, reds, yellows - all colour - was diminishing. The grey was pushing everything else out. It seemed that even the sky was getting smaller.

Even surfing, one of the things that helped him reconnect and recalibrate, felt wrong. His balance was off and seemed to be getting worse. He was constantly slightly dizzy, especially when he jumped to his feet.

Vertigo.

'I've got to have a check-up.' There was a lot going on. 'This breakup thing is really messing with me, I've gotta de-stress, or I'll make myself sick,' he thought.

The words rolled around his skull. He tried to avoid and manage stress. He knew that it wasn't good for him. It was one of the reasons he'd designed his life the way he had. He wanted to be his 'best self' and knew a job that made him stressed and took the best from him wouldn't help him be an engaged dad and husband.

He was losing his way, and his frustration was showing. He was hoping the trip would be a circuit breaker.

Leaving

He'd flown a lot recently. This flight was really uncomfortable. He couldn't settle, too distracted, uncomfortable, confused. The time stretched. The destination stayed endlessly in the future. He tried to sleep but couldn't.

His head was full of fuzz and he twitched and tossed in the seat that seemed to have too many corners. Needing to do something, he dug into his bag for a pen and visual diary. He reached for his pen. It evaded his efforts to find it. This was happening a lot. Things he'd put down five minutes before simply vanished.

'For fuck's sake,' he thought, 'the bag's not that big. Didn't I just do this a minute ago? How much longer is this flight?'

Tossing and turning again in his seat, he looked for the elusive position that would ease his discomfort.

At his accommodation, he slept heavily, uncomfortably. He woke feeling like he hadn't slept at all; as if he were hungover. The discomfort of the flight stuck and followed him through the next few days, sitting on his shoulders and directing him slightly away from everything he tried to do.

The work this time was unusually difficult, despite having done many workshops and having held lots of exhibitions over the years. Normally recognised as a very competent person in his field, he now felt like he was working in glue. Colour sucking glue. Thick, syrupy, grey glue.

Words seemed harder to find, his hands seemed slower. It was as though he was wearing thick gloves. Sensitivity to the way his hands worked was vital to his profession. The ability to judge the amount of pressure he was applying, the way he held his hand, the angles he directed his fingers, were all vital parts of his work. His brain was sluggish. Surprisingly though, some things came quickly and sharply.

His work wasn't a job. It was a passion, something he couldn't stop doing. He recognised that his life was not ordinary. It was rare to have the privilege of following your dreams, and making a living from them. It was unusual to fly in the face of societal pressure and carve a life from something so frivolous… But it wasn't frivolous.

There was pleasure from knowing that what he did contributed somehow; that his work could actually change lives in some small way. He wanted to show his children that you could do what you loved. That you could create an income that did small harm to the planet. It was possible to step outside overconsumption and have a fulfilled life.

He also knew that his job brought joy to people, encouraging them to find simpler and more fulfilling paths for themselves. Now though, it was all starting to feel wrong somehow.

Confused by the state of his relationship back home, he couldn't reconcile the path he'd chosen with the place he found himself. Hadn't he tried to live a good life? A life with some integrity? How and why did things seem to be going so badly at home?

This trip was not going well, despite the excitement and the possibilities of it. He struggled through his first scheduled obligations. Now, there was doubt about how he could get through all the coming events.

His shoe slipped from his foot yet again and the left side of his face seemed to have an itch he couldn't scratch. His left foot somehow managed to catch every little lump in the ground, sending him slightly off-balance and slightly unsettled into conversations and interactions he normally navigated with ease.

The next few days would be demanding. He needed sleep.

A knock at the door fell a long way down into his sleep. So far that it disappeared almost entirely with the distance. He heard his words return slowly through the grey towards the knock.

"Coming."

His voice was thick on his tongue, dulled by the fog of trying to awaken.

"Jeans… where are they? I need pants."

He reached for his pants, and fell face-first onto the timber floor, rolling his shoulder into the fall to protect his head.

"Crap, that hurt!" he shouted dully into the greyness of his thinking. "Klutz," he added, as he reached for the bed to pull himself up, shaking his head to reduce the fog of what he thought were the remnants of sleep.

Sitting on the bed he attempted to reach for his jeans again. His hand slipped off the edge of the bed and he fell again, grasping for something to slow the fall. This happened over and over. His efforts to stand were thwarted every time.

The invisible oil that was covering the room was too slick to get enough traction to stand.

'This is fucking ridiculous,' he thought as he slipped for the sixth time, 'why can't I put on my jeans?'

He finally dressed, through a haze of numbness and grey. The toilet was a distance away as he made his way there in a strange, uncomfortable, dreamlike state. Finally finding the door, he fumbled with his fly.

The zip was hard to find and the movements done for fifty-plus years, usually automatic, were clumsy and endless. The urgency increased. He had to sort this out quickly. Yet nothing complied. The pressure overwhelmed.

Warmth down his leg signalled both his failure and embarrassment, but also the seriousness of the situation.

The Hospital

He made the call.

The ambulance guys seemed like nice blokes; professional and caring, though the look they shared with each other when he mentioned the melanoma he'd had removed three years earlier pushed a shaft of fear up his spine.

'That nightmare was sorted,' he told himself, 'why are they interested in that?'

He watched the outside world slide greyly past the ambulance windows and made jokes to bury his concerns.

[I'm at a hospital. I think I've had a stroke.]

The text took forever to write, his fingers appeared to take their own path to the letters on the phone. Autocorrect seemed to be resisting his efforts to pass on the message to his wife.

His thinking, his world, had become even more crowded in the last few months, but now his thoughts were almost entirely a grey confusion that completely blocked his focus.

"Why does everything seem so hard, so confusing? I can't seem to get on top of anything," he muttered into the mist in his head.

The staff went about their business with warmth, unaware of this internal dialogue, oblivious to his struggle to get a clear thought through the dirty grey pillowcase wrapped around his head. The hospital was new, yet still smelled like every hospital.

"How do they do that?" he asked the grey. "How do they make every one of them smell the same?"

It was true - the smell of hospital antiseptic seemed to be designed to be slightly foreboding. It was perfumed with a hint of something like fear; a scent that was vaguely threatening, as though offering a warning. 'This place has pain, stay away!'

He was as scared as the grey fog would allow.

Wheeled around the building beneath, he was getting in the way of conversations about 'collapse', 'melanoma', 'fifty-three years old'… He was wheeled just fast enough to stay in front of the words; just fast enough to keep him from wearing the full impact of them.

Looking around, almost curiously, he took in the activity from inside a disembodied and slightly distant grey balloon pushed into the corner.

After dozens of rooms, questions and corridors, he arrived in a room with a machine in its centre. The CT scanner was impressive. It was all white, quiet and efficient looking, yet very intimidating.

Just the idea of being scanned affirmed something serious was happening. Tiny white spots of light swirled in front of the machine. So subtle they were almost unnoticed. He tried to focus on them but the fog in his brain diffused his thoughts. "Are they from the scanner?" The thought remained muffled and the question disappeared into the fog.

Afterwards, the doctor came in, pulled a chair up to the bed and sat looking at him over the plastic guard along the edge of the bed. She studied some papers, then faced him with a concerned smile.

"You seem like a straight-shooting kind of guy. There is no easy way to say this, so I'm just going to give it to you straight." Her Irish accent somehow softened the words. The white dots he had noticed at the scan appeared, became bigger, and gently swirled in the gulf between them that widened as he heard the words… "You have a mass in your brain and some lesions in your lungs. Try not to worry, it might not be cancer."

The words hit hard, though were deadened just slightly. Like being slammed with a large soft boxing glove by someone who knows how to hit.

There should've been fear, or anxiety, or something, but he was operating on autopilot. The hardness of the words, their impact, somehow didn't cause fear…yet. There was a void, a space for scary thoughts to take hold. But not quite yet. Something had to be done. He had to take steps, some sort of action, to prepare for some of the possible futures that he knew would creep into the darker corners of his imagination.

"I have to do something, tell someone." His thoughts wafted thickly through the fog. "Make sure my wife is okay, let the girls know, call someone…"

The first calls were unanswered. He left a message; "I need to speak to someone, an actual person."

The other side of the country was asleep.

Eventually, a tired croak filled the phone. A voice responded. His conversation was brief, confused. He tried to order his thoughts, to be as clear as he could, but felt the conversation twist and buckle under the pressure from the mass in his brain and the craziness of the situation.

"Hey Andy, I'm at a hospital. Look after the girls. I've got a brain tumour."

The spots of white light appeared again, swirling. His tension eased somewhat, knowing that something was done, some action taken.

He fell into an uncomfortable sleep, being pulled from it regularly by hospital noises. Moments of sleep and tenuous consciousness were brushed with images of more of the white dots, growing fractionally larger, swirling slowly.

As the night wore on, the weight of the situation settled more heavily on his shoulders.

"Fuck, I think I've got cancer. It's that fuckin' melanoma. I don't want to die like that. Fuck! Fuck! FUCK."

The fear came and grabbed at his chest. The taste of adrenaline was thick on his tongue. Memories of his father's battle with cancer shoulder-charged into his thoughts. Tears pushed at his eyes and then ran. He caught them by the fingertips, stopping them from falling. Fighting to keep control, he dug his heels into any logical thought he could, pushing back, stopping his brain from going there. 'You don't know it's from the melanoma,' he told himself. 'It could be benign.'

"It's the fucking melanoma."

The voice whispered, at first almost unheard, before it finally said clearly: "You're done. You are fucked."

"Stop, you don't know that!"

The voice then countered, arguing with itself. This internal conversation rolled on relentlessly in his head.

"You have to get on top of this," he told himself.

"You'll go mad… you'll make yourself stressed."

"You can't fight this thing if you need to… if you are stressed."

"You've got to get a grip."

He reached for his mobile. "Get that meditation thing."

The earplugs shut out some of the hospital noise as the gong penetrated the fear. The soothing voice eased through the earpieces and he felt himself soften, the weight on his chest easing. That voice was an escape from this turmoil, and he kept returning to his breathing. The tension gradually fell away.

Focussing on the present, pulling air in and pushing it out, he felt the warmth of it as he exhaled. It seemed ironic to him that something he did every day unconsciously could be an escape from this reality and give him relief from the thoughts of a future with aggressive tumours eating his lungs.

This fear had existed inside him since watching his father's painful disintegration and death from lung cancer. As he relaxed into the meditation, the white dots again grew and were joined by others. They spun lightly in the room, their presence slightly diminishing the fear that was now becoming less solid and easing its hold on his chest.

Sleep came. A beautiful, white, dreamless sleep. It was a temporary escape from the greyness of the confusion that'd been hanging over him. He woke slowly. It was like lying in a lovely warm bath while dirty, cold, grey water seeped in.

Consciousness drifted back, but as it did he noticed the greyness; those confusing balloons of grey that crowded his thoughts, had diminished slightly. The steroids were reducing the inflammation in his brain, easing some of the pressure.

It was still dark. Either very late or very early he guessed; time had been an intangible idea for a while now. The confusion caused by the 'mass' in his brain had made managing time almost impossible. He had, to a large degree, no idea what time or even what day it was.

For months now everything had been blending into an amorphous mist out of which the events of the real world emerged sluggishly, forming slowly in front of him like ominous clouds.

Introduction to "The White"

The sounds of the hospital came to him. They were clearer, somehow less intimidating. Some voices close by cut through. There were sounds of what was clearly a traumatic event in the ward. He noticed some colour in it though, and some clarity in his own thought processes. An older woman, clearly in distress, was being cared for.

"It's ok, it's ok sweetie." The nurse's voice gently caressed the older woman's fear and pain into submission. "Don't worry, we do it all the time, it's nothing that can't be cleaned up. We'll get you some clean clothes. There is a lovely nightie we can put you in while these are cleaned."

The nurse's voice was a stark comparison to the sounds of the elderly lady. While he could not hear her words, her sounds were laden with pain and embarrassment, her noises being gently met with the compassion of the nurses.

All this while the city slept, oblivious. He was taken by their efforts to give her back some dignity. He felt he knew the old lady's type. It could have been his mum. These women were tough and stoic, suffering from the embarrassment of the circumstances, experiencing more pain from the loss of dignity, than any physical suffering.

The nurse's job was to tend, to help heal. They went beyond this. There was something else here beyond just a job. Their compassion drifted through the ward.

The white lights appeared again and moved around the room, dancing softly in the sounds of the nurse's efforts to ease their patients' suffering.

He decided he would try to acknowledge these people, somehow let them know they were seen, that their kindness was seen.

Sleep returned and he fell again. Another deep, silent, dreamless sleep. The sleep he'd been having for months now had been restless, broken, and drenched in sweat. This was a relief.

Morning provided that tiny moment of respite, the micro-thought that perhaps he had awoken from a monumentally bad dream. Reality pushed hard into his thoughts when the unfamiliar feeling of the hospital bed solidified under him. With consciousness came the rebuilding of the previous evening's events.

"Fuck! Fuck!"

He caught himself.

"That won't help. Keep it under control," he whispered into the vortex of thoughts, over and over again, eventually soothing himself back to a semi-controlled state, a place where he could at least function.

The flurry of texts that appeared on his phone the second after he turned it on distracted him from the remnants of his night. Why so many texts?

The tiny white dots reappeared in the room, swirled and grew in number. The grapevine on the other side of the country sent out its tendrils. Words of concern, well wishes and love.

The white dots danced and brightened and he wept. The tears were, at first, tainted with some fear, but the white dots moved it to the side.

There it was, something just behind the fear - something bigger than the fear.

There were lights, brilliant spots of light. They were coming from his phone, coming from across the country, from his friends new and old. White little sparkles of light.

He had no idea what they really were though, no inkling that it was love… common, ordinary garden-variety, breathtaking… love.

Usually never spoken about as 'love' of course, often disguised as a simple action, never seen for what it truly was. Five minutes of time to care, to listen, to help, to be of service in some way - just five minutes to send a text. And yet there it was, in front of him.

Love.

He'd never seen this before. It danced into the room, drifted from the nurses, hovered above the hospital visitors in the form of these dots of white light. He was unsure of this. He couldn't seem to see each dot clearly. Even though the steroids had reduced the swelling in his brain, there was still a grey filter over his perception and the dots remained elusive. They were just apparent enough to attract his focus, but not strong enough to hold it. They disappeared into and out of the grey fog that kept him just out of the world.

The Irish doctor returned later that day and sat next to his bed. Her words found him through the grey. Her face was about a metre away; the white dots drifted between them, their presence strong enough to be noted but not so substantial that he could hold his thoughts to them.

"You'll have surgery on Monday to remove the tumour. It has to come out. It won't be here at this hospital. There is another one that performs brain surgery all the time. They're the best around. You'll be taken there by ambulance tomorrow. The surgeons there know you are coming. All your scans have been sent over."

She spoke gently but directly; he could feel her concern. The white dots spun lazily again. Her words drifted through the grey fog. He knew they were important but the colour in the words was muted, their meaning soupy and vague.

She left, leaving an empty chair and a void for dark thoughts to fill.

He took up the spiralling mental dance again. Thoughts of a future for his children without him were met with his best attempts to remain upbeat; to tell himself everything he could to lessen the horror of the images coming at him from the dark.

"I want to watch them grow."

"You don't know you won't, the tumour may be benign!"

"You don't know it is!"

"Who will walk them down the aisle?"

"Who will be there to help them? Protect them? Stop them from the suffering of losing their father?"

Around and around he danced, turning and reeling around the grey dance floor. Tears marked the periods he lost the ability to hold back the dark.

He turned his phone on again. The texts came. They poured in; a relentless, continual stream. He was prepared for a few, but not this. He had never experienced anything like it. There were texts from friends and workmates. Words of love, concern, and offers of help.

"How can this be?" he asked himself.

"Why? Why so many?"

He sat for a while, unsure of what to make of it. He couldn't fathom why there were so many lovely texts and so much love being sent his way.

He scanned them, looking for one from his wife.

He called her.

His family was coming.

His community was in motion. Kids would be collected from school, bags packed, people coordinated, flights booked and paid for.

They were coming.

He crumpled under the knowledge that his family was coming, that there were people, his people, out there in the world, who had his back.

He wept.

He turned his phone to airplane mode and locked out the world with his earphones, losing himself in his meditation. His mind quietened. He slept again. A quieter, white sleep.

The climb out of this sleep was slow, like emerging gradually from a cloud. The whiteness dissipated and the world solidified around him slowly.

For a period he had no clue where he was, or what had happened. When his hands were real enough for him to operate, he reached for his phone, vaguely aware of its presence on the trolley next to his bed.

The phone did its internal machinations, bringing itself to life.

The texts began again.

One after another, each one signalling more and more white dots.

The pinpricks of white swelled and danced lazily in the room. There was no tangible indication of their source, but he knew it was the concern of friends and family, and that it had travelled across the country.

It was love.

He had been slow to get a mobile phone, and even slower to get a smartphone. He hadn't seen the attraction. He had no real need… But now! He loved this machine. The messages had been coming thick and fast. More concern, offers of help and well-wishes poured out of the phone, streaming endlessly from the other side of the country.

As the day went on it became clear that he had no clue about how to deal with it all. It was too much. The white dots reappeared again and swirled, gaining in number and size. They were becoming harder to ignore. His finger found the switch and the phone's screen faded.

He needed some time to process this; time to step away from the white firefly-like dots that were now everywhere. So he talked to the nurses and made bad jokes.

At first, the interactions diminished the white dots, though they still drifted into his periphery enough to almost pull him from conversations.

He wanted to make his situation easier for the hospital staff. They had a tough job, and he wanted them to know how much he appreciated them, that he knew what they did when everyone slept and how much they gave.

The white dots gained in number, and in brightness.

He watched them swirl around the man with the food trolley as he thanked him for the meal.

"You won't thank me after you've tasted it," the man replied through a smile the thanks had created.

The standard 'hospital food' joke was a universal opportunity to bridge gaps, but this time the white dots did that, wafting between them, somehow a conversation all on their own.

Dinner was like all hospital dinners. This was one of the few times in his life he wasn't interested in food.

He forced himself to eat.

The Truth of "The White"

It was night again. The day had come and gone, a mixture of confusion, hospital machinations, fear, and thoughts.

He danced the dance of the previous nights, again trying desperately to escape the thoughts of death, his family's suffering; of all the crappy things about a slow and painful disintegration.

He wondered about his funeral; who would be affected by his end, and who would miss him.

He wondered if he could kill himself if it got too bad.

He wondered whom he could get to help him die if he wasn't able to.

These thoughts gradually built in intensity and weight, squashing out any chance at rationality. He careened endlessly through these scenarios, rolling and twisting in an effort to avoid each one and the pain and tears and snot that accompanied them.

He shook his head unconsciously as if to throw the thoughts from his mind, a silent physical scream of 'NO!' to this relentless suffering. Yet he was at the whim of something greater than his will, a process denied to no living creature.

Death sat in the corner of the room. Quietly. Just there, waiting, showing him its bony hands. Each time Death turned to face him, there was a surge of fear. A shot of adrenalin ran up his spine, pushing at the hairs on the back of his neck and almost taking the breath from his chest.

He lay in the sheets. Silent. Immobile. His chest rising and falling, heaving. His mind writhing. He tried to 'feel' the lesions in his chest, wondering how long it would be before they became unbearable.

The sensations of the plastic beneath the bedclothes, that plastic barrier, added to this cacophony of suffering, yelling at him that he was in a hospital.

His gaze raked over the objects in the room.

Hospital.

Hospital.

Hospital.

Everything said the same thing. There was nothing in this room that took him away from the fact that he was in serious trouble - in a hospital on the other side of the country.

His eyes finally rested on the view directly in front of him.

The ceiling was framed by the tracks that the curtains ran in, barely separating him from the others in the room, and again, reinforced the realisation that he was in deep, deep trouble. The ceiling was as you would expect a hospital ceiling to be, bland and indifferent.

He rolled that thought around for a few seconds before reality again hit him square in the face, the impact finding its way into every corner of his being.

Melanoma. The doctors had avoided saying that word. Their responses were, 'let's wait and see', and, 'there's no evidence to say it's malignant'.

He knew what it was. The problem was that if it was melanoma, then he thought he was done.

A version of this hospital ceiling in front of him was now most likely his future. This next, or perhaps last part of his life, was probably looking at hospital ceilings. He searched the space above him for something that defied that possibility.

There was nothing.

In an effort to escape, he began to look for himself in that space, something about him that would deny that future.

He was strong, he could beat cancer. Before he had finished that line of thought though, it was pushed aside by another.

"Your dad couldn't."

He pushed back.

He had always been a physical person.

He was fit, he surfed and he did karate. All physical things. He knew his body.

The ceiling crowded in again.

If this ceiling was his future, then that physical person he had known was probably gone. This was a slope towards weakness, pain and death.

He began to look at the person he'd been. All of the physical things that he had identified himself with were now, in the face of this, utterly insubstantial. Bit by bit, the identity he had assigned himself over the last fifty odd years began to disintegrate.

Who was he? Who was he if none of those things existed?

He felt his edges blur as the stories he had collected about himself became transparent. This process continued. He searched for something to stick his stories to, only to find that everything he had hung his identity on required a body, something tangible to carry it. But if this body didn't exist…

Who was he?

It dawned on him that he was an illusion.

He, the person he had thought himself to be, did not actually exist. He was a figment of his own imagination. After fifty odd years he'd been collecting stories about himself that constructed an identity in the world, in the lives of those who experienced him.

He was nothing more than distorted, convoluted fairytales.

In the midst of all that was going on though, he had no real idea just how profound this discovery was, and just how much it would impact him. The realisation that his identity was a flimsy construct led him to a place that was quieter and more contemplative.

He had nothing left right now. He was exhausted. There were no tears, no more adrenalin, nothing, not even his identity. He finally realised that he couldn't maintain this level of suffering, inadvertently stumbling onto an easier way to 'be' with this.

He remembered a time as a kid when he and a bunch of his mates had gone to a local waterfall. He had stood at the edge, suffering. He couldn't back out. His mates had all jumped, but he stood there, trapped, immobile, unable to leave and unable to jump. He had finally taken a breath, leaned forward, and drove his feet into the cliff beneath him, pushing his now committed body to the drop. He had surrendered and jumped.

It was time now. He had some choices. Fight. Kick, scream and resist.

Or surrender… to whatever happens.

He realised that resisting this was pointless. It wouldn't change a thing. In fact, he could see that it would make things much worse.

By resisting and fighting he would give the suffering a space to grow, and his resistance would only feed it. The knowledge followed that the suffering would not just be his; the fight would be borne by his family too.

He wanted to do this a particular way.

He could either live with integrity and grace, and then, when or if it was time, he could die with dignity and grace.

This idea gave him a surge of courage, and charged his chest a little. He was able to take some power with that stance, and it became something he muttered to the inside of his skull many times over the next couple of years.

A friend of his had lived with cancer for over ten years. She and her husband had negotiated that path with endless dignity and grace. He was in awe of the way they'd carried themselves through the process. They had now, unwittingly, become role models, and a mantra was born from who they had been, through their cancer dance.

He was also aware of the consequences of stress in situations like this. He knew that stress released chemicals and processes that hindered healing. Perhaps, if he could remain calm, he may give himself a shot at survival after all.

Live with integrity and grace. Die with dignity and grace.

He shut his eyes, took a deep breath and surrendered, completely and utterly.

He had no real identity now; nothing to protect, no position to take.

He relaxed, and stopped wrestling with the imagined.

There was no more fight, nothing left to do, except lie back and observe. Watch the world slide by and ride this ride to its conclusion.

Falling into a greater peace than he'd experienced, he reached for the phone, and searched out his meditation soundtrack just the same. Going through the motions of plugging himself into his earpieces and turning on the meditation, he finally drifted towards sleep.

In the slow fall into unconsciousness, he became aware of the white dots, moving and growing. They swirled more energetically and began merging, growing, eventually cocooning him in a beautiful white fuzziness.

The whiteness transformed itself yet again, and seemed to be moving, flowing.

There was now something else… a hint of gold running through it.

The closest thing he could think of was of an endless milky white river reflecting liquid gold. It was white and gold at the same time.

Transfixed by its beauty, he was conscious that he was studying this from an aesthetic perspective, from a distance, when the realisation hit him, rippling throughout every fibre of his being.

It was like being hit by a powerful wave.

This White was *pure, blinding*, white *love*.

The white dots he had been seeing were *love*.

It was the concern for him, from friends and strangers alike. It flowed into him, pouring through and out endlessly. This was beyond his ordinary, human understanding of love. He was filled, bleached and purified.

He was carried through this whiteness, gently, and yet at the same time, he wasn't separate. This was the most beautiful thing he had seen or felt. It triggered all of the senses he was aware of and more.

He could all at once feel, see and hear this. There were words woven through this and through him.

"You are loved."

These words turned over and over, rolling in his consciousness. He had no idea of time, no sense of travelling through it. He lay among this whiteness, adoring every moment.

He was loved.

There came a time when the sounds of the hospital woke him from that bliss. From the moment he woke, he knew that things would not be quite the same. He looked around the room, now conscious that in 'the real world' he was loved.

In the days and weeks that followed, this realisation was a bit of a shock. He had tried his best to be a good person but had often been impulsive, opinionated, and even unkind occasionally. He knew how broken he was; had seen the inside of his head. He had lived with all the insecurities, the flaws, the desires to fit in, and the poor behaviour he had inflicted on others in his efforts to be liked.

He had believed that no one could really like him; he knew what he was like. But he was loved, and in such a monumental way he could never have imagined.

Not only had the 'White' experience shown him love in a way that was beyond his previous comprehension, but it had also allowed him to see more clearly the strength of the love that others had for him.

It was a strange experience. He felt freer, lighter. He didn't have to prove anything. He was loved exactly as he was, warts and all. No more having to impress.

There was a space in the world in which he felt he could focus his energies on relationships in a much healthier way. The sense of relief was tangible. He smiled - for dozens of reasons all at once - from the core of his being, from the depths of the whiteness inside him and for everyone who had expressed their love.

He lay in his bed, considering his situation, aware that he now had a strange feeling of profound peace, despite the circumstances.

Transferred

The trip to the next hospital was less confusing than the previous ambulance ride. The grey had subsided somewhat since the last trip, allowing him to engage a little better with the ambos. The 'whiteness' had changed his focus (and, possibly, the steroids).

There was a slight sense of 'newness' about things. The steroids were reducing the swelling in his brain, easing the pressure and easing the greyness. The conversation with the ambos was every day, but he felt their concern. The white dots were clear and turned over languidly in the air between them. He made jokes, tried to pass on some of this newly noticed whiteness to them. He smiled as he wondered if his jokes were actually funny, or if ambulance officers were trained to humour their addled passengers.

The labyrinth of the new hospital was almost indistinguishable from the last. Made entirely of endless corridors and lifts, faceless people on missions, and endless rooms of suffering and discomfort.

It was newer? Had more green? He wasn't sure if these things were true or if the grey fog, which, while diminished, was still dulling and twisting his thoughts.

He watched the busyness of the staff and the hospital. He found himself noticing his reactions to his journey through the innards of the hospital, till eventually he was left in a room near a nurse's station.

There was a strange detachment in the way he observed. Much of the fear had gone. Curiosity had taken its place. He wanted to talk to people, find out about them, suddenly very interested in them and their lives. He somehow felt connected to them now, aware that the 'whiteness' was in them too.

He settled into his new room. He thought about The White experience. If that whiteness was at the heart of everything, then nothing could be too bad.

The thought earned a smile. The idea that he had a brain tumour, was possibly insane, and should probably be more scared, made him smile again.

His Family Arrives

He knew that they were near. It was late. The flight was about five hours and delayed. The ride from the airport would be slow, adding to his anticipation at seeing his family.

Lying in the darkened room, he was unaware of the endless starlit abyss surrounding and undulating with the processes of creation and destruction, oblivious to the drama being played out in this tiny corner of just another galaxy. The machine that kept track of his heart and other functions beeped at him dispassionately. He looked at the time.

The plane had landed. His family was here. His heart skipped. He wondered if the machine would notice. It would take them an hour or so to get from the airport to the hospital.

His brain engaged itself now in a different way. He was torn. He wanted to see them, could barely stand the anticipation, but it was tempered.

Things had not been great at home when he'd left.

Things with his wife were not ideal.

He wanted her here now though. The experience with The White had allowed him to see that, somehow, he had lost his compassion. He had lost his ability to deal with things in the way he once would have.

The White had shown him another way.

He saw that he could still work on his relationship with his wife. He wanted to tell her. He wanted to clean things up. Before this, the 'grey' had taken away his options, left him feeling that there was nothing he could do to save things. As the greyness diminished, he'd begun to realise how much the tumour had been affecting his behaviour. He could see how his thinking had been crowded, stifled, leaving him angry, blocked and confused. He had overreacted, lost his kindness.

This thought hurt. He'd considered himself a fundamentally kind human being. The kindness left him only occasionally, when under threat. Underneath everything, he thought of himself as kind. To have lost some of that part of himself was a shock. He was saddened by the fact that his girls had seen the worst of him; seen him in a way that'd hurt them.

Thoughts turned in his head about the girls. He didn't want them seeing him like this. He had been strong, big, capable. Their protector. Here he was now though, vulnerable, small, weakened, and in the hands of others.

How would they react to that? How did he tell them that this might be the beginning of the end of his time with them? That he may not be there later when they needed him?

These thoughts had found their way in many times since the melanoma had been discovered three years ago, and that terror had lost none of its potency.

He loved them so much. Tears dripped onto the sheets. He caught himself, stifled his thoughts and braced for the arrival of the most important people in his life. It was easy to forget what was important in the 'mortgage/buy stuff' world. Even he, who had worked so hard not to, was pushed into the path of that juggernaut.

He heard them coming and oscillated between excitement and trepidation. The faces came around the door. The first few moments of awkwardness passed quickly. The communication was simple but powerful. He looked into their eyes, and they looked back.

His happiness at being with them was all-consuming. It obliterated all the previous stories that had been rattling around in his head.

The universe pulsed, and in a tiny room on a tiny blue planet, two girls, too big to do what they did now, climbed into a hospital bed not designed for three people, placed their heads on their father's chest, and began to sing gently.

"Try not to get worried, try not to hold onto problems that upset you…"

He was transported, taken back to the many times he had cradled them, singing away their fears, making things OK… singing pure love to them.

They did this for him now. They sang into his chest, sang away his fears, returned his love. Tears poured from him.

This was one of the most exquisite moments of his entire life.

He wanted to hold them like that forever, wanted to tell every father he knew to hold their children's faces, look into their eyes and tell them how much they loved them.

The importance of those tiny moments in the night reverberated through him. He saw how magnificent a moment playing in the grass was. They weren't 'throwaway' moments. They were big, glorious moments in which profound memories were made, in which lives were made. He saw with crystal vision why it had been so important that he stood on aching feet, barely awake, to sing in the darkness, ignoring the call to his bed.

He now knew why it was important to sing that tune to skinned knees, broken friendships, broken hearts, and to tiny, general, ordinary, every day childrens' sadness.

That his children had come to him and had sung to him in that way, settled with a profound and deep warmth into his chest. They understood love. They had seen it and were capable and willing to return it. This thought was cathartic. It was perhaps the greatest gift he could have given to them... and to himself.

Day Pass

It didn't seem right leaving the hospital in this state. His new world, so far, had all been in the care of doctors and medical staff. This world was one in which he was sure he had cancer, and that it was in his brain. It seemed odd that they would let him out. The thought occurred that maybe they were letting him go because it was his last meal with his family.

Being out, free almost, was liberating, and yet…

He had been given a pass out, time outside to spend with his family, and they had decided to hole up in a cafe. He watched the world roll past the car window, aware that it was all different. It was strangely new, in no way ominous or threatening, just new. There was now a different narrative running in the background that altered the entire world.

They wandered the streets for a while, looking for somewhere quiet and warm. It was a cold and windy day, the kind that makes you conscious of your cheeks. They found a warm pub and nestled into a large nook with enough room for them all. They ordered food and fell into family banter, overshadowed by the surgery planned for the next day.

The doctors were going to remove the tumour in his brain.

He sat in the space, watching these people who had flown across the country to be with him. His wife, his daughters, and one of his best friends sat with him.

The list of the possible side effects moved through his thoughts, trying to enter the cocoon they had made around the table. He looked around at these faces and was taken with just how much he loved the beings that owned them. He deeply loved these people.

He had heard the sayings over the years about money and love, about material things not being important, heard dozens of little, trite, throw away sayings that were supposed to give an insight into what was important. Except, he realised, they weren't trite or throw away at all. Sitting here face to face with some of the futures possible to him now, these sayings were profound and deep truths.

These people were the most important things in the world. Money - stuff - just didn't compare.

He thought he had been mindful of his relationships with others, but now realised how cavalier he had been with many. Those white dots at the CT machine had come from these people and others. He loved them more now than he ever had. He wanted to hold their faces, look into their eyes and tell them how much he loved them, tell them how much they meant to him and how his life had been richer for them being in it.

This seemed a strange place to be deepening his love for those close to him, but it just proved the other line that had been thrown around as long as he could remember.

'There's no time like the present.'

He realised that *now* was always the best time to tell those he loved, how much he loved them.

They walked and explored; they stood in the wind, feeling the chill on exposed skin, delaying the inevitable trip back to the hospital. This was a moment he adored. Walking in the world with his girls was bliss.

It wasn't until much later that he discovered he'd been dragging his left foot. That he was slurring his words. That the left side of his face had slumped.

Surgery

The anaesthetist was wearing a cover over his hair with batman emblems on it. He smiled and asked his patient if he would like a gin and tonic, or something stronger.

"Something that numbs completely without the hangover please," he offered into the air and faces leaning over him.

His family were in his periphery. He smiled. He could feel their concern and see their fear. He tried a few more jokes. They worked a little. The tension softened a touch, even if it only showed itself as the obligatory eye rolls as he handed out 'dad jokes'. Despite that, he could see in their eyes that the layer beneath their responses was hard and sharp, the veneer barely covering their fears.

He waved to his family as the gurney was pushed out of the room and he descended into an amorphous void.

Expansion

In the depths of the anaesthetic haze, he gradually became aware of being conscious. And, that he was 'travelling'.

There was no sound or sensation that confirmed it, and yet he was travelling! It was like no other experience or journey he'd been on before. There was a sense of movement, but not in any linear way. No time, no distance. There was an awareness of a kind of expansion, but even that word was completely inadequate. There was an eternal, endless space, that this expansion was filling.

This was a momentous journey. He was conscious of being away from his body, away from sound and sensation, away from solidity, and yet still in it all somehow. There was nothing to tell him where he was, or anything to tell him how long he'd been there.

There was a quiet, white fizz; a subtle, all-encompassing energy.

He imagined it was like being completely immersed in a carbonated, milk filled womb. It was as though every atom that made up his body, was individually immersed in this energy, and it somehow permeated every layer of him. These layers were now expanding beyond anything he could begin to conceive.

The whiteness eventually gave way to a black, unending space. He was at the edges of the universe, and beyond. There were stars and nebulae, energies and matter, pulsing across the abyss.

He watched the birth and death of galaxies, and yet, at the same time, he saw particles and electrons moving, dancing to the whim of unseen forces.

It was the beginning of everything, the creation of everything. He was watching the lives of stars, trees exploding up from the earth, soil changing into life, and at the same time, he was 'in' these atoms, and between them.

He was part of this cosmic dance, leaping and pirouetting with the push and pull of the universe. Time and distance here were completely meaningless.

'He' was completely meaningless.

The Meeting

An immense, blinding presence became obvious. This 'light' took up the entire space in which he himself had expanded to fill. It somehow flattened him and drove him to his non-existent knees. The light obliterated everything else. The stars fell away.

The word 'being' was incredibly dissatisfying. This entity, this 'light', was everything. How could something that was everything, be a 'being'? The only word that came to him to describe this presence was **The Source**.

Woven through this kaleidoscopic experience was an immense peace. There was incredible, unending, blinding love that was beyond any he could remember, and yet, it was incredibly familiar. He was completely at ease, aware that there was nothing that could harm him.

He was *Home*.

Forming itself in the white fizz and stars were words. The communication was unlike any he'd ever had. It was more like telepathy than spoken sounds.

The 'words' were written, but they were also felt and heard, all at once. A torrent of unspoken communication, layered and understood completely. They came from everywhere.

"You are safe, you are loved completely, unconditionally."
"You are enough."
"You are forgiven."
"When you leave your body…"

> *"You will come home."*
> *"This is not your time."*
> *"You have a purpose."*

The next word was an answer to a question, answered as he formed it.
"Why me?"
"Communicator."
These words were instant, immense, larger than anything he had ever conceived, epic in scale. They were immeasurable, had no beginning or end, and came to him in a way that was astonishingly layered.

Each word meant dozens of things at once and simultaneously answered every question associated with them.

This dialogue had ingrained itself in him. It infused everything. The conversation planted itself in him, wrapping its roots around his very essence. They were not mere words. They were totally beyond 'ideas' or 'concepts'. They were now 'knowings' and 'understandings' that penetrated to the core of him and beyond.

There was nothing that came close to describing it.

He knew now that there was something behind the veil of the three-dimensional world that we were unable to see, something divine and unending. Religions had been attempting to explain this for centuries, and fallen short, allowing human flaws to pollute the reality of 'God'.

There was no evil, no 'bad', no 'devil'. There was no vengeance or punishment. These were all just human constructs; stories created to attempt to understand life.

The frailties of human characteristics were purely that. Human, and part of human existence. Under every 'thing' (and every 'no thing'), there was just endless, pure love, and divinity.

In the three-dimensional place his body inhabited, there was misguided behaviour by humans locked into survival thinking. Locked into cruelty, greed, power and status, and blind to their true nature. Behind all that though… was never-ending, rapturous love.

It was clear.

Play and give light.

That was all there was to do.

There was a purpose to life. It was a gift, a fleeting flash of experience to be savoured, tasted, and there was light to be played with. The light was something we could give away endlessly, without diminishing ourselves. In fact, kindness and generosity were gifts to ourselves.

Every time we gave our service, our time, to someone without expectation, we grew. Our light shone brighter. Kindness and playing elevated us above survival thinking. He understood now why people were so moved when they saw children playing, why our hearts swelled when we saw kindness.

These things took us home; they took us closer to the light. It was clear to him: that was our job in the three-dimensional world.

It was to shine. It was more than possible to experience the bliss of this in the 'solid' world; playing with life experience and dancing with light took us to what some would call 'heaven'.

Heaven on earth was possible.

The world wasn't solid. It was a veneer, and in the gaps between atoms was love. The world was built on love and light.

He felt that it was time to return and settled into a warm darkness, his thoughts falling silent.

Awake

The journey back from the anaesthetic was long. He could hear the voices of his family in the distance, floating quietly through the whiteness that held him. He had an awareness of trying to open his eyes. That simple task was usually automatic, but now it required a force of will. He wanted to see his family, but he felt that by returning to consciousness he was somehow leaving something wonderful. He pushed his eyes open, and as his vision widened the people he loved took shape in front of him. They were there, more solid now, and concerned. He could see that through their smiles.

He also sensed their disquiet, as they took in this man, once bigger but now small, bandaged and groggy. There was relief mixed with their worry. He had survived the surgery. They had left him just as he went under and had wandered around for six hours, waiting for news. He was unaware of the depths of their suffering.

His family had no way of knowing how the surgery had been going. They were 'out there' walking in the world, but in reality never really leaving. A part of them stayed in the room with the scalpels, the drills, and the bone fragments, the blood and the machines, and this man they loved, no matter what they did with their time.

They had filled in time, spent time, and killed time. They distracted themselves from the ugly possibilities until the promised phone call. The voice filled them in. He was out of surgery. It had gone well. They left some of their concerns lying on the grass in the park and headed to the High

Dependency Unit where he would recover.

The operation had gone like clockwork. Possibly one of the advantages of having been reasonably fit and healthy. That, of course, and the fact the surgeons were highly skilled. They'd done their work well.

The family had to know. Would this man remember them, would he be able to talk, eventually walk? Was this the beginning of his disintegration, a cancerous descent into the ground? What would their lives be like now? They needed reassurance, and they needed to reassure him, this man whose life was intertwined with theirs in the most intimate of ways.

This father, this friend, this lover, and more. Would these roles continue? Or be the same? He pushed out muffled words as his family tenuously formed and faded in front of him. They told him they loved him in the gaps that were left between the nurses tending to him, and the remaining spaces where he was conscious.

Unconsciousness pulled at him, dragging his eyelids further down, slowing his words and thoughts. His family left as he again fell in slow motion, back into the quietness of the stars.

Awakened

The gentle clattering of the tea lady's trolley, and her soft words that followed, lifted him slowly into the world. "Would you like a cup of tea?" He looked up into her eyes, gradually firing up the functions to answer the question. The tea was spectacular, though in reality, probably nothing special. To him it was glorious. He looked at the tea lady and the others in the room, each busy playing the roles that circumstances had imposed on them.

These other humans were different.

Everything seemed very different.

He couldn't immediately pin down why. He tried to sweep away a little more of the drug-induced fog. There was softness with people that he hadn't seen before. They were somehow less substantial. He thought about this for a while.

As each person entered the room, he watched, mesmerised by them. They were softer. There was something missing from them that in no way diminished them, yet at the same time something was added. In fact, they were now quite beautiful, gentler, and at the same time, less fragile. It seemed like a contradiction.

"What had changed?" he wondered.

He dug around in his head trying to find the point of difference. These people didn't look like that the other day. He took these thoughts, and his view of these people, apart.

They were indeed different. He became aware that they used to have a shell of some description, a facade that was blocking the view of something else. The 'shell' that he had once seen wrapped around people was now diminished. It had become less substantial, transparent. He could see right through it.

He had never seen people this way before. That shell was the way he had seen them in the past. He could now see something beneath, something that shone. This light he hadn't seen before either. These people glowed from within; a sublime light beneath the veneer of skin and bone.

He wrestled with these thoughts, tried to make sense of them. The haze of the residual anaesthetic and the awe at seeing people like this was clouding his ability to comprehend it all.

The day passed, punctuated with trollies, clipboards, pills and busy nurses. As he searched around in his brain, trying to reboot parts that were sluggish, he began to become aware that this new way of seeing people was not the only shift that had occurred. It was as if something had been downloaded into him.

He was back in the real world, and yet noticed an overwhelming sense of peace and ease in circumstances where he knew he would've responded differently 'before'. Much of his fear had disappeared, and the entire world (the hospital) now seemed less substantial, not just the people in it. Everything seemed slightly dreamlike.

Despite trying to separate the two 'places', the edges between them were blurred. There was a thin skin of three-dimensional reality that made up the entire world. There was the 'solid', superficial world. But it wasn't solid. Under that, was something else. There was another dimension beneath the appearance of solidity. Everything seemed to blend into everything else. The edges of most things were like looking through a lens that had been faintly smeared with Vaseline.

Paradoxically though, everything was, at the same time, clearer and not at all blurred.

As he continued to watch the goings-on in the hospital, he became surer of what he was seeing. The outward appearance of everything had become softer, allowing a light within to shine. He found that he could focus and see the light very clearly. People were light-filled beings, and the 'people' aspect of them had faded.

He considered the white dots that had swirled around the room and coalesced around him at the other hospital. That light was here now - it was them, all-pervasive and all connected.

The light was these people.

This thought hit him like a sledgehammer.

This had been explained '*There*'.

Everything was connected. This light was at the heart of everything. He had come across this idea before and even considered it may be true. Now, however, he sat in a profound and glorious understanding that it was actually, monumentally true.

It was the beginning and the end of everything.

It was beneath everything, and in it, everything was connected.

Every.

Single.

Thing.

But it was particularly concentrated in life, and even more particularly, consciousness.

The presence that had spoken to him was this light. Our purpose was to awaken to this. It was to be conscious of our animal nature, and rise above it, rise above selfish and primal survival thinking. It was to be conscious of our light.

Some words popped into his head: '*Play and Give Light*'.

Our purpose is to play and give light. It was now SO clear.

Playing and giving light are the ultimate forms of gratitude for the gift of life.

Kindness, compassion and generosity were expressions of light.

It had been communicated to him in 'the light', but this, now, was a physical realisation that light was the one thing we could give away that didn't take away from us; in fact, it was the one thing we could give away that 'grew' us.

What the hell had happened to him? He was a bit confused. This place, the one with the pain and the edges that had seemed so real to him before, was now less so. The 'other place' was much more real. The memory that he had been somewhere washed over him. He couldn't place exactly where or when, but it was definitely during the surgery. The more he attempted to make sense of this new view of the world, the clearer he became.

He had always been a talker and was usually comfortable with his ability to explain and share concepts and feelings. Strangely, despite his increasing clarity, words were now completely inadequate to express this new knowledge. Adding to the strangeness of having all of these understandings, was that the entire experience had been rapturous, and its residue was still with him.

As time progressed, more and more insights about what he had learned would make their way to the forefront of his consciousness.

The ordered chaos of the hospital occurred around him. Patients and staff all involved in their own version of reality moved through his. Sometimes they merely brushed past, glancing off the side of his world, and other times landing squarely in it. Each interaction was different, no matter how fleeting.

He could 'see' these people with much more clarity. He felt a stronger connection to them. In a way, they were all similar to him. He 'knew' them now. At their source was **The Source**. Their ego was just a facade to help them survive in their world. The face they showed this world was a veneer, designed to hide, or show, pain, fear, and anything else their body had decided it needed to survive.

Underneath though was light… endless, eternal light. He could not help but love them; these beings, inside these people, like him, were light. They normally existed in a state where time and distance were irrelevant, but for the moment, they lived in these bodies.

Had they forgotten who they truly were?

He wondered about that. He considered the possibility that all others knew about this and were playing a game. Perhaps he was the only one who was not awake, and the 'others' were testing him. He sat in his bed laughing quietly to himself with that thought.

The Phone

His phone had become something incredible. Not only was it his lifeline, a vehicle to speak with the ones he loved, it was also a way in which he could receive love. These were simple messages from his friends. Tiny pulses streaming through the air delivered through everyday technology, and yet they were more, so much more.

They were something solid to hold onto. They gave him light.

He knew he should be more scared, he knew he was now in this '3D' world, aware of being very small. These messages though, some short, some long, some just a photo, lifted him. When hard thoughts came to him, like dying with cancer and seeing his children suffer watching him, the messages softened them.

He was not alone. There were others who would walk with him.

These simple, beautiful messages made this experience somehow greater than he could have imagined. Those couple of seconds that someone took to contact him had the most incredible effect. There was peace in those pulses that eventually arrived on his phone's screen. He wanted the senders to know their impact.

The phone though was becoming even more than that.

He had never considered himself able to write. Spoken words had come to him reasonably easily, written words not so much. Now, the words came flying from his fingertips and poured onto the screen. They came from somewhere separate, from somewhere 'other'. Somewhere without thought.

It occurred to him now what it was the hospital staff actually did, how they transcended their 'jobs'. There was more than the bedpans and the dispensing of medicines. There was love, service, kindness. This unseen love often happened in the dead of night while the rest of the city slept.

There was something radiant about many of these men and women. He couldn't write, could he? The words came thick and fast:

> 'You are not just nurses; you are not just doing a job.
>
> We want you to know who you are for us.
>
> You are the soft voice in the night; you are kindness in a time of pain and fear.
>
> You are reassurance when we are alone.
>
> I have watched you serve, I have watched you tend & care.
>
> I have heard your compassion when the rest of the world sleeps.
>
> You are not just doing a job. We know… and we want to say thank you.
>
> Thank you from the bottom of our hearts. I will never forget who you are. I thank you.
>
> ~ A patient.'

The High Dependency Unit

The High Dependency Unit was a warm bubble, despite the seriousness of the situation. The nurses checked on him regularly, somehow infusing the simplest request or conversation with warmth and kindness. He was getting used to the routine. Every three or four hours, tests were made to make sure the disrupted pathways in his brain were working as they should, and the machines were checked.

It was a joy when the nurses came by. They had fewer patients than the general wards and were able to indulge him with stories about their lives.

He loved these people and loved each one anew as they changed shifts and routines around him. At one point he had his own room, close enough to the nurse's station to be able to hear about their weekends and outside lives.

Sitting quietly, he listened to their voices, picking out each personality, smiling and wondering whether they knew how much they were sharing with the ears in the closest room.

Nightmare Ward

He watched the hospital slide past. There was something said about the High Dependency Unit needing a room, so he was being moved to a new ward upstairs.

The new ward felt wrong.

There was something about the place that sat awkwardly inside him. There were two others in the room, one opposite and the other next to his bed. There was something about this space, something ominous and oppressive that hung over the room.

He struck up a conversation. The man opposite had lung cancer. It was in his bones, his pain accentuated as he made the effort to leave the room for a cigarette.

In the smoker's absence, he lay for a while, thinking. He'd tried to look after his own lungs. Having watched his father smoke when he was a child, he'd heard the coughing every morning that brought him to his knees. He'd watched his father quit smoking, seen his struggle to step away from that addiction. Watched him become incredibly fit to avoid the consequences of smoking for so long.

Eventually, though, his father succumbed, finally dying the death he feared.

After all this, smoking was not going to be his choice. He hated cigarettes. It occurred to him how ironic it was that he was lying in a hospital with tumours in his own lungs, while the dying man opposite went for a smoke.

That night, he overheard the smoker's conversation. He was speaking to a visitor through the pain of cancer destroying his bones, his words clipped and altered by the discomfort.

The room was dark. The man's son had come in to visit. Their voices, though soft, still travelled across the room. Without knowing it, despite the words he used, the man gave an incredible insight. In the half-light of the room, in the last two weeks of the smoker's life, he heard the man speak to his son.

"Whatever you do, don't let the fucking bitch drive the Jag."

These words would echo through life for him. Until the smoker had said these words, he thought this was his future. He realised he had a choice. Cancer or not, that was not going to be his future. His life was more than a car.

The smoker's conversation, his concerns, seemed bizarre. They seemed indescribably ridiculous. How could you be lying in bed, in agony, facing your final moments, and worrying about 'the bitch scratching the Jag'? How could a car be what you were worried about? His words added to the already palpable oppression in the room.

He heard the overweight man in the other bed move and grunt over the jarring sound of the TV.

He had to escape this room.

Tentatively putting his feet on the floor, he tottered into the hallway to escape for a while.

As he re-entered his ward the smoker spoke up. "Didja see the size of that bloke in the bed next to you?" Without waiting for an answer the smoker continued. "He's gotta be a hundred n' eighty kilos, you should see the size of his arse. It's fucking huge. He can't even walk. It's fuckin' gluttony if you ask me. He can't stop putting stuff in his mouth and he's too stupid to know it's killing him. The greedy prick broke his foot and he's so fat they can barely operate."

The irony of his words was lost on the smoker. He seemed completely oblivious. The smoker could've been talking about himself.

He couldn't listen to this anymore. He needed to get out of there, and away from this place as soon as possible. He forced himself to climb back into his bed and put his earphones in. The meditation track settled into his thoughts, dulling the dark ghosts in the room.

Death Is A Battlefield

It was late and very quiet for a big hospital full of people. He'd been woken by the smoker, his low moans of anguish sitting heavily in the gloom and adding to the darkness. As the man's tortured mutterings pulled him to consciousness, the weight of the space came with it.

The smoker was in the last stages of lung cancer. His bones were breaking down with the disease, causing unimaginable pain. The sounds were involuntary, squeezed from him by a massive hand that wrung his body slowly and relentlessly.

Lying in that room, he watched the curtains being drawn by the nurses that almost silently appeared. Their voices were muffled, but didn't soften the hell the patient was in, and were loud enough for him to get a sense of what the smoker was going through.

He was on a precipice here. It was easy to fall into the depths of his own predicament; easy to see his future and to careen though his memories of friends who had walked the cancer path. Wallow in the horror of having seen his father break down with cancer. It was easy to put himself into the bed, and the man opposite, with all his pain, sweat, anguish and fear.

His thoughts turned on him and he heard the internal voice ask: 'Why me? Do I have to do this revolting, hideous dance? Why me? It's not fair.'

Fear appeared, grabbing the back of his neck. Tingles of cold were forced up his spine, pushing against the base of his skull. He felt himself tense. His chest tightened and sweat ran down his armpits.

The fear, though, was quickly followed by a moment of silence, and then by an almost tangible feeling of expansion, before he answered his own question.

'Why not me?'

This question shoved him sideways, out of his fear. He was transported back through time, looking at humanity's evolution, at lives and deaths over centuries.

How many millions were ripped to pieces by animals? How many starved slowly to death? How many froze? How many women died painfully in childbirth?

He then considered humanity's role in death.

How many millions of brothers and sisters, mothers, fathers, had died slowly in the dirt? How many in battles? In holes? In the blood and in the organs and excrement of people they themselves had been hacking into only moments before?

How much pain had they endured? How long had they suffered? Had they felt their lives ebbing away, felt their consciousness slipping from their bodies as they lay in the filth and blood?

And that was just humanity.

How had the deaths of zebras, seals and other animals been at the hands of predators, disease and the environment?

Why not?

Why not him?

Why should he be different, special?

What right did he have to expect an ending that was soft and gentle and painless?

The history of life would say the odds were stacked against that.

He swam futilely in this eddy for a while, trying to keep his head up, trying to reconcile that he was probably in for some serious pain at some point. He found some traction, the eddy slowed, and then it came; there came some clarity…

Life equals death. No life, no death. No death, no life.

This glorious experience of being able to feel the sun, of being able to love, to breathe, to hurt, to live, was part of a deal. His puny life had to end. Everything did. So what if it was from cancer? At least he got to say goodbye to those he loved. At least he got to clean up his crap and apologise for his weaknesses and indiscretions. How many were denied that privilege?

Stars, planets, civilisations all ended. It was part of the deal of being alive. Death equalled life. They couldn't be separated. To resist death was to resist life. This was a monumental process that had been going on since the beginning. Every living thing would end in its physical form, and, if truth be told, would probably end in a painful and unpleasant way. If he was to die from this cancer, there wasn't anything special about that. It was just the way things were. He could see that now. The only thing that could be special would be how he lived in the midst of this. Now that would make a difference.

There was a place here that was free from the fear of suffering.

He was still not keen to endure pain, but he could see a way that he could make living with cancer useful. This idea had come to him earlier, and now settled deeper into his mind. He felt out the corners and sharpness of the situation, and came back to the possibility that he had discovered earlier. He could live with as much integrity and grace as possible, or, die with as much dignity and grace as he could muster.

These words went deep. He wept in the bed.

There was some freedom here, a possibility that excited him. He had a larger purpose with this future, whatever direction it took.

The Whiteness pushed into the fabric of this place he now found himself. Words emerged, coming from him this time, and gave light to a room that had been very dark:

"Happy to stay, happy to go."

When he looked at this, he realised he had given up his attachment to his life being any other way than the way it was right now. He was free from the suffering of worry about the future. In this headspace, he could really, truly live, despite the circumstances. In this headspace, he could truly, deeply, be alive.

In this moment, his relationship to pain and suffering changed. A great peace descended on him. It was consoling to know that he was just doing life like everyone else and that he was part of a timeless process that was meant to be; the epic process of destruction, recycling, of creation itself.

He wasn't separate, he was connected in this way to all living things. He was not only part of life, he *was* life; he *was* death, he *was* creation.

This put his life in a different context. It now seemed much less important that his body endured. It was just a small collection of elements that had come from the stars, coalesced for a period, and would one day return to the cosmos, just as it was supposed to. He felt another layer of himself fall away. He felt any remaining fear he'd had about dying dissipate, ebbing away with the remnants of his fear about living. He was free.

The space that opened up with this new context was massive. No fear of death? He began to realise just how much of his life was tainted and manipulated by the fear of death.

The greater the fear of death, the greater the fear of living.

He became aware of just how insidious that fear of death was; how much of the experience of life was affected by it. So many things were impacted by the urge to survive, and in ways that were not readily apparent. The lines between what was a genuine fear of dying, and what was an imaginary fear, were blurred. Things that once appeared to be serious threats, became puffs of smoke. He found himself smiling. Many of these threats were actually completely ludicrous. He chuckled at just how ridiculous it was that he had allowed such stupid, tiny concerns to get in the way of the miraculous possibilities of his life.

Losing his fear of death was all very well though, but that 'fear of pain' thing was still there. He had seen cancer, seen the suffering first hand. He wasn't keen to suffer that much.

The words, 'Happy to stay, happy to go' re-appeared. And again, the endless blissful peace came. He marvelled at the depth of this feeling. What was going on here?

There was no resistance, no struggle, no fear, no suffering, and in the void that was left, a depth of peace that was breathtaking. He sat outside his thoughts, no longer attached to their babble. He just watched, looking at the meanderings of his mind, amused at their wanderings and yet not affected by them. They were just thoughts, nothing more. They did not need to be acted on, they didn't need to be stopped, they didn't need to be taken on. He could just watch. He had surrendered to what was, and now there was just silence.

This earned another quiet chuckle. How long had he been at the whim of his thoughts? He had been drifting around through his precious life at the push and pull of his own brain farts. It was laughable. He wondered if this quietness was temporary. Could he maintain this state in the face of what may come? The rarely silent voice sitting at the back of his skull chimed in. Often the things it said were also brain farts - counterproductive, feeding into that whole fear dynamic that took him away from his experience of life - but this time, it quietly said, "That's the future. It doesn't exist. Come back to now." And he felt the slowly building concerns drop away as he settled into his bed… in the silence of now.

Visiting hours and his family eventually arrived. Their presence lightened the ward. His youngest daughter jammed herself next to him in the too-small hospital bed and forced everything else in it into submission. The others left. He and his youngest watched a movie together. He looked at her face, so close to his, and remembered the cuddles, the tears, and the glorious insignificant moments they had shared.

He could still feel her tiny head on his chest from when she was small. He had read to her when she was little, could still see her little eyes wide and wandering the page, bathing in the magic he was pulling from the little black marks and pictures. "Splosh went the frog!" It was a line from a book that appeared in their lives even to this day, sparking conversations that brought smiles to the whole family. 'How precious were those memories?' he thought. In the past, he tried to hold those moments close because he knew they were important. But now, in the face of this new, possibly short, future, they weren't just important or precious, they were everything. He now understood that in those moments, he had been face to face with **The Source**.

He vowed to never take those moments for granted again, even if he had fewer left.

He looked again at her face, as it rose and fell with his breath. A smile came as the memory of her first dance class pirouetted into his thoughts. She had wanted to dance for a long time, and his wife was working so he had been the parent on duty. He took her to the venue; she held his hand and dragged him in. The closer they got to the music and pink leotards, the less she pulled and the more he did, her nervousness slowing her and transferring from her sweaty palm to his. There was the threat of a child's 'moment'. This bit of parenting was often not so much fun, and almost as terrifying for him as her first dance class was for her.

He sat and watched the other kids dancing and whispered in her ears the words he thought would get her onto the floor with them. She was locked between his legs, arms wrapped around his waist and the back of the chair with her head wedged under his arm. He persevered for a while, eventually realising his words had no power and he finally surrendered to her shyness.

Sitting for a while, he braced himself for his next attempt. He took a breath and took her hand. He led her onto the hall floor with the other kids. He was a terrible dancer. He always felt awkward dancing at the best of times. Despite his lack of coordination, he was actually almost enjoying it. Not the dancing particularly, but the recognition that this was one of *those* moments; unpredicted and seemingly small, but with great power and lasting consequences.

Holding the hand of his baby, he eased her into a new world, guiding her through the process of facing her fear. The other kids loved this awkward giant, stumbling among them.

He loved being a dad, loved being *her* dad.

Finally, the little hand tugged at him. "You can go now, Dad." Just like that, he was out, temporarily no longer needed. His smile stretched wider as he thought about how she'd been dancing for over seven years now.

Running his hand over her hair and cheek, he felt warm with the glory of that moment. The TV and the movie called him back. In the movie, metallic ant-like creatures were making scratching sounds on the tiles covering the walls of a lab. He felt his daughter move to the highs and lows of the movie, enjoying his arm around her. This was a good way to get over the trauma of having your skull opened at least! In movieland, the bad guys were defeated and peace returned to the television.

His wife and other daughter returned. Eventually, visiting hours over, his youngest extracted herself and left with the family as he talked himself into taking on what was apparently food, and even less apparently, a pork belly. The veggies, at least, still looked like veggies.

There was more television to watch. The imagery of the universe and some of its more convoluted components were explained in the way only Stephen Hawking can. He was mesmerised. Apparently, gold had been created in the depths of space and spewed into the cosmos as the star that created it exploded in a monumental tantrum, almost as impressive as the one he'd dodged at the dance class all those years ago. Through billions of years these fragments collected with space dust, other elements and possibly some alien belly button lint, and formed our tiny planet. Incredible. Wedding rings came from the stars. He fell asleep.

At some point in the night, he awoke. He had no way of knowing the time, other than it was somewhere between the regular nursing observations. He guessed it was about 1 am. The lung cancer patient across from him was still in pain, making noises that signalled the difficulty of getting air into his diseased lungs. Again, the dark possibilities of his own future rose.

He fought the thoughts. While his recent experiences with The Whiteness had given him some respite, it was difficult to escape the nagging suggestions inspired by the tormented sounds of the other patient's breathing.

The large man next to him had fallen asleep while watching Japanese anime cartoons. The lurid greens and pinks stained the room, flickering and changing, casting surreal lights around the already oppressive atmosphere. The primal growls of demons, monsters and battle added another level of weight to the mood. It was too much. All this overcame his efforts to hold it together. The fear crept up his back and he tried to bury his head in the bed to hide from the nightmare miasma of sound, colour and thoughts.

That mistake earned instant regret. He had momentarily forgotten the thirty-eight staples in his head that held the large flap of skin closed. He'd jokingly asked the neurosurgeon before the surgery if they actually used a hole saw to cut through his skull. The 'yes, we do' response had been interesting and slightly amusing at the time. It was neither of these things now. He winced as some staples caught and pushed the fresh wound into the small gap cut in the bone of his skull. It would supposedly, eventually, form some kind of fibrous net over the gap, but now it was very fresh and raw.

The pain was a temporary escape from the imagery, which had been charging around his brain, triggering one nightmarish scenario after another. It was a blessing in some ways. It pulled him from his imagination and threw him sharply into the present. He had to get out, get up. He'd heard one of the surgeons say that fitter people can have lung problems if they lie prone too long. He was reasonably fit, and not prone to lying still. He told himself, if ever there was a time to get up, it was now, regardless of the time.

Raising himself unsteadily, he put his feet on the floor. The nightmare dialogue masked the tingle as his feet touched the cool vinyl. His instability was now very much at the forefront of his mind. Fear of the room and the thoughts forced the first step. He took it, then another, and moved tentatively out into the hall. There was no one at the nurses' station. He unsteadily set off down the long empty corridor, taking tiny steps, determined to put as many as he could between him and that room.

After shuffling some distance, he came to a darkened part of the hospital which, to his mind, seemed older and unused. There were doors that were closed. His imagination was now barely contained and he had the sense they were shut for sinister reasons.

One was open. He eased himself in, his curiosity overcoming any common sense. His eyes adjusted and he noticed a chair of some description resting ominously in the centre of the room. It was a cross between a chair and an operating table, its shape somehow openly threatening. He had the feeling that bad things happened there. That the chair held nightmares. He shook his head like he could shake out the thoughts that were scratching sharply for attention. The shake offered a fresh burst of pain, reminding him again that he'd very recently had his skull cut open. This thought brought him back to the chair. What had happened in this room? What was done to people here?

Barely managing to control his fear about his future, he was now trying not to add images of cutting and flesh and steel and sharp things. The thoughts dropped on him relentlessly, one after the other. An horrific, inescapable mental torment. They became stainless steel insects creeping around from the corners of things.

The fear of going back to the room was still greater than the nightmares that were starting to appear in this one, until the metallic insect thoughts transformed. They became spiders with slim, cold, sharp metal legs. They clinked and scratched their way out of the dark corners of the room where the eyes of the ones controlling them hid. He scrabbled for control, barely hanging on. He knew this was his imagination. He knew that he was full of steroids and a chemical cocktail that was designed to manage the surgery and its effects. Despite this, the fear still crept up the back of his neck like one of the spiders, towards his staples, lifting the hairs on its way, feeling for an entrance.

He imagined its sharp feet making its way to his freshly stapled wound. The posters on the wall took his attention. He hadn't seen them before, but their discovery grabbed him and threw him over the edge, gasping for air as the adrenalin shoved air through his lips. The pictures were medical pictures of dissected eyes, opened, staring, prized apart with long metal claws. Claws that looked like the ones being wielded by these spiders.

The hospital was silent. His heart raced as he headed for the only light source in the room, the open door.

Despite the clutching, scratching wall of fear cascading through him, he could only make small footsteps. A flashback to a distant nightmare about being chased bombarded him. In it he'd been running as fast as he could and yet went nowhere, screaming without sound. He'd woken the whole house.

In this part of the hospital, he was alone. Alone with his thoughts and the sharp, cutting, prying creatures. The imagined metallic clattering of the insect's claws sent him shuffling into the now endless corridors, back towards wherever his bed was. He came across something familiar, and eventually found his way to his room. He climbed into bed as fast as his injury and balance would allow. He reached for his bedclothes, pulled them over his head and lay there in the dark like that, panting, tears squeezing through eyes clamped tight, pulling any rational thoughts towards him and trying to keep the spiders and the creeping, scratching thoughts out of the space under the sheet.

Finally getting some clearer space in his thoughts, he managed to calm himself down by slowing his breathing. Reaching for his phone and earphones, he searched for his meditation tape. The lurid glow of the television next to him was still casting its disturbing hue around the ward, tainting everything with its flashing sickly green and pink light. Like bad special effects in some B grade, poorly made horror film. He had to deal with this, now. He knew he couldn't endure an entire night.

Glancing across to the large patient who'd been watching television, now fast asleep, he realised the remote had fallen to the floor. Sucking in a breath, he lowered himself to the floor and crept under the curtain, fumbling for the off switch. The sickly flashing of colours ended, leaving the ward dark once more. The action helped banish some of the crawling thoughts, and he climbed back into bed feeling strangely proud of himself; something so simple disproportionate to his sense of victory.

The eye pillow shut out the world, and he mopped up the remaining residue of the experience by dropping into the world of his meditation tape. It was safe there.

"There is only now. Nothing else exists."

He wielded that mantra, each time shaving small slices from his fear and eventually reducing it to something manageable. Focussing on being present brought some of The White, and he fell raggedly into a disjointed sleep before finding the stillness of deep sleep.

The hand reached out of the hospital gloom and into the silence of his sleep. Despite being woken, the routine was somehow reassuring, soothing. A voice quietly joined the hand.

"It's time for your Obs."

Looking through the gloom, he smiled at the new face. The next nurse had taken over from the last and went through the now-familiar questions and tests of hand and leg strength. The accent and the face greeting him were wonderful. There was a kindness in his eyes that sparkled, even in the low light. He braced himself for the worst part of the ritual. The tiny torch was switched on and its beam swept across the curtain, coming to rest in his eyes. It was a shock every time, the tiny beam like a house brick thrown at his retinas. He recovered from this assault and his eyes re-focussed.

He then went from the hospital's routine to his. He was determined to know each nurse's name, partially because of his newly reinforced admiration of them, and partly to acknowledge what they did, to pass on some light. In addition to trying to rebuild some of his cognitive function. He knew that his brain was damaged, and he should probably start rebuilding some neural pathways. He wanted to test his short-term memory.

This nurse's name was Operakesh. Opi explained he was originally from India, and suggested we should use the name Opi, for simplicity. Opi's nature could be felt in the darkness. He instantly liked him. The conversation flowed easily in the predawn and drifted to his recent experiences of the Whiteness and some of his discoveries. Opi smiled at the words, somehow understanding what was being said. There was no hint of cynicism or disbelief. His smile just grew in the darkness, felt rather than seen.

Opi promised he would bring back socks that matched the hospital pyjamas. They laughed in the dark at the concept of Opi worrying about matching socks only days after major brain surgery. It seemed ridiculous to be concerned about socks after having had your head opened and things poked in there, cut in there; after having a part of your brain removed.

"You are young," suggested Opi. "You should take time to look after your appearance," he said through his smile.

He laughed up through the plastic barriers on the side of the bed and countered, "I'm older than I look."

Opi took the bait. "Okay, how old are you?"

"I'm fifty-three," he said, wondering how many birthdays he had left. His efforts to guess Opi's age were way off the mark.

Opi was sixty-eight.

'Sixty-eight doing this job, and walking around the hospital at this hour, that's impressive,' he thought. He tried to look through the soft light and through his own smile, yet saw no hint of Opi's age.

Opi finally said, "Tomorrow I will bring some clean pyjamas and matching socks, and you will have a shower." He paused, a secret smile playing on his face. The smile of a parent who knew what gift a child was getting for their birthday. "It will be the greatest shower of your life." Opi sparkled knowingly and paused again, allowing the words to travel and land, then continued. "Before I leave, let me tell you a story, my friend."

His words moved softly through the darkness. He could just make out the smile on Opi's face.

"Some twenty years ago I was taken to hospital after a massive heart attack. I thought I was going to die. After the surgery and when I had recovered enough, I was wheeled into a ward. As I entered the ward, all the other patients in the room clapped and cheered. Those that could stand, did. I asked, "what's happening, why is everyone cheering?"

Opi paused here, the knowing smile slowing his words.

"One of the patients approached me and said, 'we are welcoming you to this group'. 'Which group is that?' I replied. The man took me by the forearm and looked into my eyes, and said, 'this is a group of people who are finally awake'. He said… 'Welcome, Opi.'"

Opi paused in his story, stood silently for a few seconds, watching the words land in the consciousness of the man lying in the bed. He finally moved and picked up some things in preparation for leaving to tend to other duties.

Before leaving, he moved back to the bed, gently wrapped his hand around his patient's forearm, and looked deeply into the eyes of his new friend. In that soft light, Opi said some of the most beautiful words he'd ever heard. "Welcome Mark, welcome."

Opi smiled knowingly and walked out of the ward and into the hall, leaving him in his bed, weeping and convulsing with joy. When he slept, it was in the all-embracing peace of The White.

The New Room

He loved this room.

His wife had organised for him to be moved to another room. This one only had one bed, its own bathroom, a window, and a view straight to the nurses' station.

It was a relief from the darkness of the previous ward.

There was so much more light in here.

The Shower. A Journey To....

He rolled himself to the side. Funny how something that he'd done a million times was now a new, but slightly scary experience.

"It's just a shower, it's just a bloody shower," he told himself.

That thought was immediately met with others.

"Crap, I wonder if the floor will be slippery. I can't hit my head."

Visions of his feet sliding out rushed at him, clear and vivid. It's not something he'd worried about before the surgery. He pushed aside the image of an eggshell collapsing. The grey that had polluted his thoughts was gone. It was a relief to have that 'greyness' taken from his head, but the shock of the colour his imagination now added to the images rocked him slightly.

He knew he was still not thinking as sharply as he should - things were still slow - but the colour and contrast were there. The consequences were dramatic, making the threat of a fall even more concerning.

Smiling at his thoughts, he noticed how erratic they were, but also how much of that inner dialogue had lost its power.

He now seemed to be able to see these thoughts from a different place. They were just thoughts, nothing more. He was free to engage with them as he chose, and they no longer held any real sway over his feelings. He went back to the business of getting himself clean. It had been a while since the surgery and he really needed a wash. Opi had brought towels and new hospital clothes, making sure to place the matching non-slip socks on the pile.

Sitting on the edge of the bed, he tentatively lowered his legs to the floor. The weight of his feet on the ground was familiar, but at the same time, a different experience each time. He was unsteady. This instability was new to him. While he had always been a little clumsy, he was robust, six-foot and strong. He was used to bouncing off things, used to ignoring minor bruises and cuts. It was collateral damage… part of the cost of throwing yourself headlong into life. The words of a friend popped into his thoughts.

"*The thing I like about you Mark, is you don't know you can't do stuff.*"

It was true, sometimes because he was too lazy to do some research or preparation; but more often because he just couldn't wait to throw himself at things. His enthusiasm often overtook his common sense, but he always seemed to escape relatively unscathed. He had always launched himself into things, looking for a safe landing place (or creating one) well after he was committed. It had always left his father slightly bemused; he'd been a very meticulous man. His father had planned, measured and considered his own actions carefully. His son was confusing to him, slightly impulsive and shambolic, a lot like a large puppy.

Despite the difference, his father had been proud of his son. Nothing was said directly. That generation did not praise lightly. It was a sound, here and there, or a look. Not much, but noticed just the same.

Standing was something he had only done perhaps a dozen or so times since the surgery. Every time he had stood in the last few days had left him in a strange, unsteady place. This trip to the shower even more so. He could no longer rely on his strategy of leaping in. He had to plan. Where were the handholds? Are my arms strong enough to support me if I fall? Will I react fast enough to protect myself? These were unfamiliar thoughts.

He realised how much he had taken his body for granted as he took his weight on his feet. This was the first time he'd stood without the hospital issued non-slip socks. It was just his feet and the floor. There was a faint sensation of pins and needles as his feet eased around the texture in the vinyl. He was testing its nuance, testing to see how he would manage this interaction. It was beautiful, strangely new. He was reasonably steady. The floor had enough traction and solidity to ease the voice in his head.

'Now for a bigger step,' he thought as he gripped the plastic guards on the hospital bed. There seemed to be a huge smile in his head, which made it to his face. He was a driver, driving a body. He was aware that this was truly the case. He observed himself intently, smiling, observing his thoughts. There was no fear. Wonder was there. The sudden awareness that his new companion, The White, was just there in the background, made everything wonderful.

"You okay?" asked Opi.

"Yep, I'm right," he replied, smiling as he launched himself into the gulf between his bed and the bathroom.

The seat seemed slightly comical at first. It sat in the shower recess, a strange haven on the wet tiles. Its representation of safety seemed slightly ironic, given that he may well be far from safe. He had cancer. The tumours sat in his lung, quietly growing. This chair reminded him that all was not well. On its own, it was just a chair. But what it represented sitting there waiting in the shower, was confronting. It was weirdly comical, and yet slightly threatening.

He watched those thoughts appear, and rotated them in his head, looking from all the angles he could. Detached, yet alert. He smiled again, noticing how his fear of the melanoma was gone. What a huge space that left in his thinking.

Undressing, he organised his towels and clothes. He enjoyed this in a way he never had before, the fabric brushing against his skin and hands. He'd never realised just how beautiful folding a towel was. Dropping his hospital pyjamas on the floor, he smiled at the sensation of the weight leaving his hand. He noticed in intimate detail the sonic nuance as the fabric left his body, slipped past his skin and hit the floor.

Making the journey across the tiles, he felt every step, consolidating each footfall and moving to the next. It was unnaturally slow but in no way tedious.

Lowering himself into the chair, his nakedness became even more obvious to him. He noted that his nudity, his vulnerability, seemed amplified by the reappearance of the tumours in his thinking, but the sensation of placing himself on the chair took him away from that again.

He was alive.

The White he'd experienced was felt, just there, just behind the wall, in the wall, in everything. He smiled again.

He reached for the showerhead. It was attached to a hose. Turning the taps, he adjusted the temperature. The warm water rushing past his fingertips was also alive, pulsing over his hands. His breath caught. This was magical. Why had he never noticed how beautiful this was? Was it always this exquisite? It felt like someone was pouring liquid silk over him. He felt every single drop.

Was this new understanding of things somehow exaggerating his perceptions?

Perhaps it was the drugs, or maybe being face to face with his mortality was giving him a new appreciation of simple things. The 'divine mundane'; a term used by a dear friend.

He had, in the past, been aware of the magic in tiny moments, but not the Divine. He had known pleasure in them, but not this.

Nothing like this.

He knew it now.

This was Divine.

He turned the water towards his face, being careful to avoid the damaged side of his head. The sound of the odd droplets that broke away and landed on the plastic bag covering the site of the surgery was like music. The rivulets of water ran down his body, following his chest and stomach, forming a small pool in which he sat. Like a child, he tried to seal the small drain holes in the seat with his legs and backside, hoping to deepen the puddle.

The experience was intoxicating. He looked around the room, taking in his surroundings, noticing every nuance, every texture and surface. His eyes were pulled to the stainless steel handrail, one of the many safety handholds that grew out of the walls. The water spray and droplets clung to the closest one, the light gleaming on each drop, creating tiny rainbows and sparkles down the length of the stainless steel.

The image of gold being spewed into space from a dying star, and accumulating around a ball of space dirt that would eventually become earth, crept into his thoughts. He realised that this everyday stainless steel handrail, at some point, also had its elements formed in the depths of time and space.

The Shower Abyss

In that moment, and with that thought, the world shifted. An invisible galaxy-sized semi-trailer shoved it sideways. In an instant, he became blindingly aware that the stainless steel had originally come from the timeless pulse of the cosmos. The cosmic soup had coalesced over millions of years until eventually stars had been born and died, galaxies formed, planets and asteroids. He became acutely conscious that this room and everything in it was a culmination of massive cosmic events on a colossal scale, over a period he couldn't begin to imagine.

This moment here, now, was miraculous. Everything in this room was miraculous. Himself, everything, and everyone else; everything that ever existed was miraculous. What were the odds of the circumstances occurring to create this moment and everything in it? Incalculable.

As he wondered at this he sensed the walls around him becoming less substantial. They appeared to become transparent. Through them he saw tiny dots of light that gradually became brighter, the spaces between the dots becoming darker. There was the sensation of waking in a chair, on the edge of a roof of a tall building, but without the fear. There was only wonder as he tried to assess what was going on.

The walls melted into blackness, broken only by those pinpricks of light. So much so, that he was left untethered in the void of space, looking at the machinations of the universe. There was a sense of a crackling undulation of energies and movement. The intense pinpricks of the stars were witnessing this event like a crowd in a darkened theatre, the spotlight on the naked figure in the plastic seat. This experience was like no other in his life. He had the profound sense that he was again with '**Something/Someone**' and that it was showing him this for a reason. There was a divine purpose to this experience.

This was somehow a collective knowledge, a vast and timeless understanding that he had fallen into, stapled and diminished. He sat on an everyday plastic chair in space and understood the machinations that had occurred so that he was alive. The absolute miracle of his being became vividly clear. He was completely conscious of the miracle of his existence, of the room's existence, of the monumental gift of life, the life of his loved ones, and the monumental miracle of the planet on which he lived. This understanding was laden with gratitude.

As he fell through space, arms spread to take in as much of the experience as possible. He became epically grateful for every nuance of his life and everything in it. Underneath even this, beneath the immensity of the universe, there was something more.

There was a sense that this was part of something even beyond the stars, that there was a plan that had been in place since before time began.

He heard his internal voice, becoming very conscious of his thoughts. There was the feeling that now he understood how his body had arrived at this time and place. He could understand, in a limited way, how stars had been formed, galaxies built; how all these things had conspired to create him and everything around him. All these things were, in his mind, explainable to an extent, but there was still a question sitting deeply at the base of his thoughts.

'*The*' question quietly pushed and weaved throughout the tangle of synapses, making its way inevitably towards the front of his thinking. He heard his thoughts processing this kaleidoscope of realisations until they abruptly stopped. Quietness took over and he sat paralysed.

'*The*' question finally emerged. He asked it, pushed what had been lingering in his periphery, so huge and almost too big to ask, to the front of his thoughts…

"Where did this voice come from?"

From that, other questions emerged.

"Who am '*I*'?"

"What am '*I*'?"

In the moment of asking, everything transformed again. The void that he was falling through gave way to the increasing light of the stars, their colours growing brighter, intensifying, and combining. They merged, and became The White. He was blinded. This light penetrated him to his core, touched every nuance of his being. It rippled through him like a river. He felt as though he was being dipped in the stars themselves. He'd never witnessed anything so beautiful.

Tears of joy streamed down his cheeks. He sobbed, almost breathless, no longer aware of the chair, the room or the shower. This White was the same he had experienced during the surgery. This time though he was wide-awake, and the experience of it was unencumbered by unconsciousness and anaesthetics.

This endless White was love. Pure, unconditional, blinding white love.

The only words that came close to describing this were '**The Source**'. The word 'God' somehow didn't resonate. This puny human label was hollow. It was a diminishment of what he was experiencing.

He knew that this '**Source**' was behind everything, in everything; that he was part of it and it was part of him. It was in everyone and everything.

It was clear, this was everything, and he was not separate from it, could not be separate from it. This body he walked around in was temporary. He now completely understood that he was timeless; a 'traveller' of some type before being in this body, and that he would 'travel' again.

Time and distance were illusions; human constructs designed for a physical world. He now knew that his true nature, his true form, was nothing like his body. He knew that the physical was no barrier to his true form. He was part of, and yet at the same time separate from, everything. In The White, it became clear that all of humanity, all beings, *everything*, were energy; all light and all love.

We appeared, to our survival-focused minds, so separate from one another, but we were in reality linked; beings of light, insubstantial, indestructible and endless, our energetic roots penetrating through the three-dimensional experience. We'd lost sight of our essence, lost sight of the currency that we were designed to deal in.

He'd believed before these events that he should be as kind as possible, that he should try to help others as much as he could and be kind to the planet. He knew now, in a way he had never known before, that his purpose and all of our missions on this planet was to be of service to others, to give kindness, to give love. It was to trade in light. He had seen the spots of light exchanged between the nurses and patients, he and his loved ones and friends. It was even generated by the concern of strangers. He knew that this light was our true nature, and kindness and compassion were powerful ways of re-connecting.

Kindness and service, or light, were the ultimate 'currency' of **The Source**. This currency could easily traverse the country, the planet, and the entire cosmos. He had physically felt and seen the light and love from his loved ones and friends over 5,000 kilometres away. He realised that most of the apparent differences between himself and others were purely an addition imposed on us by our animal-ness and our desire to survive on this planet. He now knew that time on this planet was a fleeting, tiny experience, and that one day he would leave his body and go home. Home to **The Source**. Home to love.

His consciousness was timeless.

This word, '*home*', this revelation, caused another flood of tears. His chest hummed with happiness. He would one day go home, go to pure, blinding, unconditional love. He had a strong sense that he was not alone, that there were others with him. He had a sense of them as individuals, of their faces and mannerisms. They were people he knew. Each one appeared or was felt in this Whiteness. There was something in these faces, in these friends' essences. They shone. The faces appeared one by one and in groups, in rapture. He was mesmerised by this expression. He had never seen or felt such pure, ecstatic joy before.

One by one, the images were infused with a wordless message:

"I am *so* happy, everything is okay."

He sat in The Whiteness in rapture, oblivious to the water running over his body. He was again bleached, purified, forgiven, enough. *Loved* totally. These things he now knew were not explainable. The three encounters with The White had explained everything he needed to know, but the language he possessed was completely inadequate to even begin to describe the experience. There was the profound sense that he had somehow been deliberately shown something, that there was a purpose to these revelations.

Slowly, The White seeped away. The feeling of complete ecstatic wonder did not.

The world returned.

The whole experience had taken only moments, but he felt again as though he had been on an endless, epic journey. There was a feeling of déjà vu as he remembered that he'd been there before, during the surgery. They were additional realisations to the information downloaded into him during the procedure. His head swam trying to process and pinpoint everything. Giving up, he allowed the waves of bliss to pour over him until the shower's drumming on the bag covering his head, and the rivulets of water running down his skin brought him back to his weight on the chair in the bathroom.

Opi knocked, his voice quiet through the door.

"Are you ok?"

He answered, trying to get enough power into his voice to reach Opi on the other side of the door. "G…good." The word was husky, barely formed. He turned off the water and sat quietly in the puddle on the chair, putting together the resources to return to the world, to stand and dry himself.

This world with the shower, with cars and trees and people, was no longer solid. This three-dimensional world became even less substantial, and the energies behind everything more 'real'. Just under the surface was something else, woven through the stars and us, the thing that connected everything. There was love, indescribably beautiful, no holds barred, neverending, love. **The Source** of everything, in every time.

Opi was there as he opened the door, a benevolent force.

"How was your shower?"

Still damp, he stood in front of Opi, smiling, crying, unable to speak.

Opi gave an equally radiant smile in return and simply said: "I know… I know."

The time and everyday events in the hospital were smeared together, creating a seemingly singular experience in which he could not separate individual events. Moments were now saturated with wonder at how the world appeared, then separated by the even more glorious moments with his family and new interactions with the hospital staff. He noticed that time had ceased to flow the same way as it had before. In The White, time was irrelevant and not linear. There was an essence of that leftover, making it hard for him to put events into a timeline.

He rolled onto his back and looked at the ceiling, listening to the nurses tending to his fellow patients with incredible compassion. His thoughts drifted to the Irish doctor he'd met when he first presented at the hospital. There was something there, something he'd discovered about himself as she delivered the results of the CAT scan. He noticed his concern for her. She'd turned up to do her job and was given the task of delivering this bad news. His concern had him trying to make it easier for her despite his situation. He hadn't imagined that he would do that in those circumstances. It pleased him to realise his first response had been compassion.

His interest in his phone had changed. In the empty moments that hospitals give there was time to think. Thoughts, insights and ideas appeared and reappeared. This device gave them an escape from his head, putting them in the real world so he could dissect them, push them around, and look at them from a distance to formulate them into 'something'.

Many of the thoughts were about processing his future, particularly now that the world seemed so different, but others were about the generosity from his friends and others. People were incredible. Someone once told him that if you want to know about people, look at the news, and watch for the helpers. With every tragedy, there are always helpers. The smile squeezed a solitary tear as he thought of the faces of his friends who had leapt to help. There really was magic in the most unexpected places.

He tapped away at the screen, poking at letters with one finger, in the way that adults do and teenagers roll their eyes about. Words turned into sentences. Entire streams of thought appeared in what seemed like seconds. No thought for the quality of the writing, and no understanding of what he was doing other than attempting to convey his new realisations. His friends' actions influenced some of the letters that filled the screen.

He had been the recipient of incredible kindness. It had to be documented. He had to record their actions. They were heroes, their actions selfless, genuine and instant. They had to be acknowledged. Perhaps their actions could inspire.

He had to write this down:

"Imagine there was a light created in the depths of the stars and the beginnings of time. Imagine that it was moulded over millions of years, crafted and shaped by the pulse of **The Source.**

Imagine that this light was indescribably spectacular and that its brilliance had the power to transform lives, to shine light into the darkest of darks.

Imagine though that that light was hidden in front of our noses. That it was missed in our efforts to survive. Now, imagine that when that light shines to its fullest extent, it would transcend suffering, and exist in rapturous wonder at the miraculous nature of the universe. Adoring the experience of simply being.

Imagine that behind all the noise, the striving and thoughts, there is that light, and that light is…

You."

He looked at the small square of light. All this stuff had poured out of him, through his fingers, to the light from the screen.

The White words he had heard and seen before now returned, leaping sharply into focus, covering him in goosebumps and running a shiver along his spine. He was barely able to hold himself up, wracked with paroxysms of joy and tears.

"*Communicator.*"

It hit him just how layered this word was. This was his purpose, to communicate about the light, to encourage kindness; to help others enjoy their lives. It was a condition of him remaining here; this was why it was not his time. He had a job to do.

If nothing else, he could at least facilitate acts of kindness.

The Test

It was several days after the surgery. The physio had him out of bed, standing in front of her. He'd been doing the exercises she asked, unsteady but upright. His feet felt 'new' but were strangely familiar at the same time. Toes gripping the floor, he'd always enjoyed the sensation of having his feet planted. It gave him a sense of strength, of solidity. Now, although he was up, he was still unsure. While his confidence was growing daily, his connection with the ground was still slightly tenuous. The ground was less solid now.

He was confident in his ability to heal, but this was big stuff. This was something larger and more confronting than he'd ever dealt with before. Someone had opened up his brain.

Keen to get on with rebuilding himself, this new project of regaining mobility was a distraction from the distant idea of his cancer. That he may not have much more time.

The physio looked him in the eye and told him she was about to push him. She shoved first his left shoulder, then his right. He turned each time and rebalanced.

"Good, this time I'm going to push you over."

His wife exhaled loudly, shocked by the thought. Moving away from the bed, he braced himself. The physio shoved him in the chest. Something amazing happened. The years of karate practice kicked in. He felt himself fall back to the left. Muscles fired. His left leg pushed into the floor and his core engaged. He felt his body correct and straighten. Still upright. Still standing. He wobbled slightly and smiled. This was a victory, a small but monumental victory. This moment signalled the beginning of his healing. He now had a say about how he was going to mend himself.

Cancer or not, he could at least be mobile and get himself stronger and fitter. He could rebuild himself in some ways to take on the challenges of dealing with the tumours. This was one first real step in the direction of living.

The physio was smiling too.

"You can leave. We had to make sure you're reasonably stable before we let you go." Her smile was a celebration of that moment. She knew how big it was for him. Thanking her, he sat on the bed, his cheeks starting to ache with the smile that wouldn't stop.

He was getting closer to home.

Leaving The Hospital

The drive to his accommodation was otherworldly. Someone he knew, who'd helped him come to Western Australia, had gone overseas and given his family the use of their house. He sat in the car, carefully examining everything. He had a vague sense of the threat that was in the background, but this was almost completely stifled by the experience of looking at the world through his new eyes.

Trees were no longer 'just trees'; in fact, everything that was alive took on a subtlety, an aspect that he had never consciously noticed before.

There was light coming from everything, so much so that he couldn't understand why he hadn't noticed it before. It seemed that everything alive was new, illuminated from within, shiny somehow. But more than that, he was now completely aware that there had been a monumental and almost immeasurable sequence of events that had led to everything he was seeing being where it was now.

Each breath he took was a culmination of an almost endless series of cosmic and planetary convolutions. It seemed that he was firmly encased in miracles, acutely aware of the presence of the stars and **The Source**, while sitting in the passenger seat of a Toyota.

The Next Day

The sound of the piano filtered in through the thick, soft blanket and pulled him from sleep. He got his bearings. The bed was incredibly comfortable. This was no hospital bed. There was no plastic crinkled beneath him, or sides to stop him rolling out. No 'Obs' every three hours, no sounds of suffering from other beds. There was only warmth, and the sound of his daughter playing the piano and singing quietly in the other room.

There were other sounds too. There were the sounds of a family going about making breakfast. A general ambience of domestic industry. Plates clinking against cutlery and glasses against the bench and bottles, muffled slightly by the soft voices of people he loved.

He slowly sat up and processed the room, the sounds that cartwheeled over each other and over the carpeted floor towards him. He put his feet on the soft floor, pushed himself up carefully, and moved unsteadily towards the familial music. A large mirror gave him a glimpse of himself, the bandages, and the half-shaved head. Shuffling and thin, he was still wearing the green hospital pyjamas. He'd been reluctant to give them up. They were surprisingly comfortable and somehow reassuring. They reminded him that there was a team of people who wanted him to get better and still worked hard for him to do so. This reflected shard of himself nudged him back into the real world (although he no longer knew what that was) and the quiet sounds of his family pulled him back into heaven.

His mother had flown over. One of his close family friends, who'd also come to help, had moved in with his family for a few days. He was amazed at the generosity of people. This house, this *home*, had been given to him selflessly to use. They were all together in a haven. He ate the most spectacular breakfast that ever existed, and sat with the warm flavour of his family, glowing with the sense of normality it gave him.

The idea of a good coffee flooded his taste buds. It'd been a while, and though the neurosurgeons and staff at the hospital were world-class, the coffee definitely was not. This was one compulsion he was determined to indulge. He announced that he was heading down to the corner where a small cafe squatted. It sat strangely in the middle of suburbia at the crossroads of two small streets, smugly knowing that a decent coffee would pull in the addicts for miles around. It was never empty.

After assuring the others he'd be fine, he launched himself away from their concerns and at the cafe in slow motion, pulling away from the house, from safety, almost the same way a lunar module disconnects itself from its delivery vehicle for the first time. The hood of his jacket was pulled over his head. Other people's reactions to the staples, and the healing wound, had taught him sharply. He'd never had people openly stare at him that way before. That there were possibly millions of people in the world who lived their lives that way evoked his deepest empathy.

It was just a short walk but different from any he'd ever experienced. He noticed every footstep, every ripple, dip and difference in the road, every sound. On the one hand, he had to observe the world in order to keep himself safe. He was still unsteady and walked slowly, being particularly vigilant about staying upright. On the other, his attention was wrenched by the incredible beauty of things that he'd barely seen only days before. There was a flavour to the air, a colour in the light, a feeling of the breeze against his face. The world fizzed with vibrations of energies.

He was alive; more alive than he'd ever been in his life.

Walking into the shop, he noticed the girl behind the counter had served him only a week ago, before all of 'this'. Smiling, he ordered his coffee. He found himself looking deeply into her eyes, crossing some normal social barriers in the process. She wasn't unsettled by this stranger's gaze - in fact, she held it and smiled back.

There was a connection. He'd seen something deeper than the superficial in her, and deep down she'd seen it in him. She, like all of us, was a fellow traveller. A sister, a brother, light, and a dealer in light. She was the same as him. She was energy, somehow stuck in a temporary form that (among other things) could make a good coffee. For a millisecond there was a sense of recognition between them, before she went back to the warm machine with its alluring smell and carefully prepared his drink.

With the warmth in his hands, he sipped slowly. "Holy crap, how good is coffee!" The words bounced around inside his head as though they were kids who'd just been told they were going to the circus. There were lists of things he really enjoyed before the surgery. He was starting to realise some of these could now be enjoyed even more completely than he could have imagined.

Coffee was definitely one.

He saw that just about everything he experienced now would be 'firsts'. Pondering this in between the warmth of each sip, when he really thought about it, there were two groups of 'firsts'. The initial group were in some ways obvious, but not really firsts. He'd lain next to death, all sterile, dry and bony white. He'd talked to him in the dead of night, in a hospital bed on a plastic mattress, with death's clean, white ribs, poking him at the site of the tumours in his lungs, wrapped in his bony arms, just to make sure he was aware he was near. For a while, he'd been sure he was going to die fairly soon. A year, tops.

The realisation earned a smile; that for a period into the future, there would be many things he'd already done and enjoyed, things he imagined he'd never do again. They felt like 'firsts'.

The second group were, truly, 'firsts'. The coffee, as an example, was definitely a first. This was the first time he had experienced coffee with his new way of being in the world. In fact, it was the first time he had truly, ever, tasted it. Pretty much everything he did, since the first meeting with The White in the hospital, was a first in this category. There was an almost euphoric enhancement of senses, and it was magical. Doing everything was magical, and for the first time in his life he felt what it was like to really *do* something.

Everything was wondrous, shiny, and made all the more intoxicating by the knowledge that he knew what was behind it all.

A world full of this was perfect.

How ironic that death had very generously given him the gift of being deeply alive.

'Going out' was unlike anything he had experienced. The world was incredible and remarkably beautiful. He was particularly taken with other people. They were no longer just 'other people'. They were extraordinary; they were all fellow travellers who found themselves in this place, with all its restrictions and all its pain. He felt he could see their lives in this three-dimensional space, cast on their faces. He felt at the same time empathy and understanding for their particular brand of human discomfort, and yet awe and wonder at the majesty of their true form.

He had a sense of the light within them.

Drawn to make eye contact, he wanted to connect. He thanked them for anything he could, smiling and laughing with them. He could feel the light he gave them and felt it return to him. It strengthened the line that connected them all to the pool of light that was **The Source**. He now actually loved people. He found himself sitting quietly, watching, smiling, and feeling the light weave through these interactions.

His job had been about understanding shape and form, concepts made possible by an understanding of light and colour. As magnificent as that experience had been, as much joy as that had brought him, it was nothing compared to this. There was light shining from trees, from birds and from people. He basked in it.

Some 'others', he noticed, had very little light. His thoughts were taken back to the nightmare ward. He knew now what was wrong with that room. There was very little light.

It was clear that beneath everything there was no 'good' or 'evil'.

There was only love.

So how did that explain the Hitlers, the serial killers, the paedophiles? He knew that they weren't evil, not from the devil. Evil, the devil, 'bad'; those were human creations, human labels. Impositions over our true nature, so the sack of skin and ego could survive. The 'bad' people were just damaged humans doing what their egos, unresolved trauma and stories about survival told them to do. They had no clue that their light was inhibited. Certainly, it seemed they didn't have the slightest clue as to what they were distancing themselves from.

He felt such sorrow for that situation. Though all of us allow our light to dim to varying degrees, he realised that one of our highest purposes is to give as much light as we can. By doing so, we open ourselves to being able to develop a relationship with **The Source**. He felt a profound sense of sadness for others who weren't experiencing what he was now.

The light he saw being swapped and intensified between people, even with just a simple act of kindness. Just a tiny act of compassion made the light dance. It was from that place that it was possible to stand in this world and live with joy and wonder.

Now, it was crystal clear that we're all dealers in light. We can all give light to others, and by doing that, increase our own. It's a transaction that transcends physicality. It's the only thing we can give away endlessly, that doesn't take anything away from us. We get caught up in the physical machinations of earth and forget our ability and power to give that gift.

It occurred to him that perhaps many religions were initially built on this concept. They'd lost their way and been caught in the sticky webs of survival thinking; power and ego. Many had stopped being about kindness, stopped being about light and about love.

It became obvious that our path is simple. We were to play and give light; to embrace the experience of life in all its complexity and wonder. Considering that he was pretty sure the melanoma had metastasised to his brain and lungs, this was ironic. The doctors hadn't said that definitively yet, but there seemed to be a clear subtext.

However, his every breath was like a fine wine. He wanted to do the dishes and mow the lawn. There was divinity in the mundane. There was glory in the simple.

It was too easy to take the life experience for granted. He considered the documentary he'd watched in the hospital. Stephen Hawking had explained the origins of gold and in fact most of the material that had gone into constructing this planet. Earth had taken millions of years to create, and the conditions for life to begin had taken a further multitude of inconceivable events and millions of years. Reflecting on all of this, he observed that at some point a slug had crawled from a swamp and eventually, he existed.

All this had taken billions of years, against impossible odds.

Before his tumours, he'd been expected to wander around for a paltry eighty-odd years. Given the multitude of events and years that had occurred, to create now, every footstep was an incredible culmination of chaos and construction.

What a gift, to be here, right now.

What an even greater gift, to be here, now, and *conscious*.

Why wouldn't we be doing cartwheels whenever possible? Why wouldn't we stand in the rain; watch bugs, slide down hills, laugh and celebrate the monumental gift of life?

Even the crappy bits can be a gift. He loved being alive more than he could've ever possibly imagined, vowing to enjoy as much of the rest of this experience as he possibly could.

He also noticed that while he adored this life, he was happy to leave it too.

He didn't *want* to leave his loved ones, but was now completely accepting of the fleeting nature of this physical existence. They would miss him, but that would pass quickly in the scheme of things. He knew what was next. Eventually, he would be with them in The White, in the eternal bliss of complete and unconditional love.

His Girls Return Home

The taxi's arrival was imminent. It's funny how waiting for a taxi in the past had been so mundane. But now… He noticed the warmth of their skin as he kissed them goodbye. They were going back to an empty home. To fend for themselves, for a little while at least.

It had all happened so quickly, a team had to be tacked together to handle some of the logistics of feeding and moving around teenage girls. His friends back home volunteered to pick up the slack. Their generosity was incredible. Though he was saddened by them leaving, at the same time he had some concerns about them coping with all of this. It was a lot. He remembered how difficult it was for him to deal with his father's illness and couldn't imagine how it was for them.

As the taxi drove away the tears tracked cool lines down his cheeks. The wind blew coldly through the trees and across his face. This hurt. He hoped it wouldn't be long.

He loved them so much.

Getting Out And About

The occupational therapist and end of life counsellor made their way into the house. They made themselves comfortable and proceeded to assess his abilities. Both in terms of processing potential 'death stuff' and the possibilities of building new neural pathways to get back some cognitive function. The most challenging part of that was the O.T.'s suggestion that he design a meal, and go shopping to purchase the ingredients for that meal.

He instantly felt his brain slow as he processed the weight of her request. After a moment, he was able to think about what he wanted. For some reason he wanted chicken and vegetable soup with barley. The barley was important. He had no idea why.

Plans were made to head to the nearest shopping centre. The centre was bright, new, clean and *loud*. It wasn't busy - but for him, it was a lot. The muzak, colours and smells. Each, in turn, slowed his brain incrementally.

Clutching the trolley's handle, he fought it into a straight line down the aisles. He chuckled to himself. *'Why is it, after brain surgery, I would pick the only bloody trolley possessed by the devil?'* It required all of his physical and cognitive abilities to even drive the thing. It was a blessing and a curse. While in some ways it was holding him up, it was also punching him repeatedly in the brain, every time it veered into a shelf. Which was often.

He was right on the edge of shutting down but persevered, looking at the list and hoping one of the items would materialise in front of him. A woman moved up the aisle with purpose - aiming for a spot somewhere just past him. This extra piece of information threw him over the edge. He shut down. His brain stopped dead. He needed something solid. He needed to sit down, but tilted into the cool security of the edge of the fridge to gather himself.

The neurosurgeons had suggested that he would probably have a fit at some point in time. He wondered, through the haze of his stopped brain, if this was it. He stood like that for an unknown amount of time, his wife finding him staring vacantly down the aisle, unmoving and leaning against the milk fridge.

"Are you all right?" she murmured, concerned.

"Sit… down…" was the best response he could manage.

This was his first experience (but not the last) of his brain dealing with the consequences of having a piece removed. He realised at this point there were going to be some challenges ahead.

Despite the chicken and barley soup event, his new version of the world meant that he enjoyed leaving the house. It became part of their routine.

He and his wife walked into the cafe. No one took much notice of him, but those that did smiled warmly. It was in stark contrast to the woman he had startled at the shopping centre earlier.

They'd gone to get something to cover his head. His hooded jacket was too hot to wear all the time. While he hadn't had a good look at the wound yet, he did know that he probably shouldn't walk around in public with it exposed. The front view gave him no real inkling of the extent of the surgery. After seeing the reactions on the faces of those that had, he'd decided a covering was definitely for the best.

He moved off to the side in a quiet part of the mall and removed the hood, beanie in hand, ready to make the transition to it as fast as possible.

There was a sound to his right. A woman stood with her mouth open. The sound he'd heard was literally her lips parting as her jaw dropped. He looked at her and smiled, hoping to soften the experience. It didn't. She stared, unable to pull her eyes from the side of his head.

He smiled again, yet she couldn't make eye contact, instead dropping her gaze and scurrying away. It was a strange experience, and gave him a small insight into the lives of so many who live with scarring, or something that makes them appear different. He'd been largely unaware until this point, but this encounter highlighted what had been done to his body.

Having his head opened wasn't a small thing, but he really hadn't thought about just how extreme the surgery had been. Hunger poked him in the ribs, distracting him, and they headed for somewhere quiet, a reward for having dealt with the mall.

The café was a haven after the shopping centre. It was only a short drive from the house. Quiet and warm, the café staff were now used to seeing him, and had an idea of his circumstances. It was incredible how people were to him now. The shocked woman at the supermarket was an anomaly. He tried to pinpoint exactly why others were now so soft, gentle and caring. While it was probable that they could tell that he had been through something, there was something else that shone through the interactions; something to do with him, and how he related to them.

The surgery and potential diagnosis left him completely stripped back, exposed. He had no defenses. He could not rely on his physicality to protect himself, even if he had few opinions he was willing to defend. There was nothing to argue about, nowhere to stand, no position to take, except in the light with **The Source**. He was liberated from having to justify or protect anything. The feeling was incredible. Despite his instability, he was light as a feather. The whole world had become softer, less sharp and solid. He guessed that while others were aware of him being unwell in some way, that wasn't the reason for the change. He surmised that it was who *he* was being that was creating a space for others to also be open.

Having shed almost all of the 'survival thinking', he was now sharply conscious of the true nature of others underneath their own survival thinking. The light was really the only thing we should be focussing on. Humans were truly beautiful. All of the reasons he'd disliked humanity in the past he now understood to be manifestations of that survival thinking. Ego and status were just about survival on earth. He could see through this now and respond to others, light to light, dancing with their flames.

He reached for his phone and tapped away, lost in the words:

```
         "I met death the other day.
           It wasn't what I thought.
It wasn't wearing black and it wasn't holding a
```

scythe.

It came to me, immense, ominous, grey and hard. It came on a screen and, from the mouths of doctors, said CT, lesions, tumours… Cancer.

I looked deep into its presence though and found a kindness there, an unexpected gentleness.

It took my hand, smiled, and threw me tumbling through the abyss, falling through the heartbeat of the cosmos.

It showed me something. It showed me the illusions I am, my insignificance… and magnificence. It showed me endlessness and divinity.

It sat me at the face of creation.

When it was done, it placed me lovingly, gently, back in my life and sat patiently next to me. It smiled and, with its grey dry hand, gave me the most monumental and wonderful gift.

It placed in my hand, with more love than I knew possible, the child anew, innocent, unknowing, unformed.

I am again, in many ways, the infant, fresh-eyed, full of wonder, full of possibility. Reborn again in heaven on earth, now, smiling, sitting side by side with death.

•

I met God the other day.
It wasn't what I thought.
It was wearing black and it was holding a scythe.

It came to me, immense, ominous, grey and hard. It came on a screen and, from the mouths of doctors, said CT, lesions, tumours… Cancer.

I looked deep into its presence though and found a kindness there, a gentleness that was breathtaking.

It took my hand, smiled, and threw me tumbling through the abyss, falling through the heartbeat of the cosmos.

It showed me something. It showed me the illusion I am, my insignificance… and magnificence. It showed me endlessness and divinity.

It sat me at the face of creation.

When it was done, it placed me lovingly, gently, back in my life and sat patiently next to me. It smiled and with its endlessly loving hand, gave me the most monumental and wonderful gift.

It placed in my hand, with more love than I knew possible, the child anew, innocent, unknowing, unformed.

> I am again, in many ways, the infant, fresh-eyed, full of wonder, full of possibility. Reborn again in heaven on earth, now, smiling, sitting side by side with God.
>
> I am."

He caught his wife looking at him often. The look was one of slight concern and mild confusion. Who are you? Seemed to be the question that came with the look. It was not normal to look at trees, birds, people, cars, everything, with rapture and awe. He smiled as he realised how it must seem to her, particularly as he'd behaved so strangely before all of this.

***

They were back in the house and settled into the lounge overlooking the river. His wife had taken a photo of the side of his head to send to his sister. He was curious. He hadn't seen the site of the surgery. Its position at the side of his head only allowed a glimpse of staples and a shaved patch.

The effect on him, seeing it, absolutely stopped him in his tracks. Thirty-eight staples and a horrific wound curving around his right ear, up to the top of his skull and back down towards his back. There was no illusion here. This was major. This was no simple wound he could shrug off as he had with most others.

He had to recalibrate. The sight of the wound coupled with his instability, and the effects of the surgery, dealt his view of himself an unblockable realisation. He reeled.

"Holy crap. Holy crap. Holy crap. Whoa… that's, that's…"

The words fought themselves to get out, eventually tangling in a pile at the back of his throat. He took a deep breath in, clearing his head and the backlog of syllables that had jammed. He almost couldn't believe what he was seeing. It was a testament to the resilience of the human body, a testament to the skills of the surgeons, but it was his head.

'A tennis ball would easily fit in that hole,' he thought.

It was at once intriguing and horrifying. While he was feeling incredibly lucky to be standing here, there was a sense that he had been violated in some way. Someone had had their fingers in his brain.

Noticing his thoughts, he looked at them from a distance. A deep belly laugh began in the layers within him, beyond any that could be seen. It eventually made its way to his face and he laughed at his thoughts. His concerns were completely meaningless and farcical; hysterical in this new context.

In the face of what he knew now, everything about his brain surgery, cancer, his concerns about everything, his puny life, were as funny as hell.

The Results Clinic

It had been over a week since he'd left the hospital. They arrived back for the results of the surgery. The Results Clinic would answer some questions.

How much had been removed?

Did any tumour remain in the brain?

Was there any bleeding?

Was it malignant?

It was amazing how quickly his wife had found her way around the hospital and around the city. In every city, there is always a parking spot somewhere that is the holy grail, particularly around hospitals. She'd found it on an earlier visit and managed to find it vacant each time, close to where they needed to go. They parked and he walked from the car, no longer shuffling, but still unsteady just the same.

Despite his rapidly recovering balance, he still looked very carefully at the ground for anything that may cause problems. He even found himself looking at the terrain for an escape route if a car came around the corner while he was crossing. How high was the gutter? Could he get between those parked cars? How stable was that post? Could he lean on it? He couldn't help but notice the thoughts. In the past, so much was automatic about moving through the world. Now, it was thought out and planned.

While these thoughts about physical safety were new, it was the absence of other thoughts that really intrigued him. There was a huge space in his thinking. A quietness that he hadn't really experienced before. For the week or so he'd been out of hospital, he'd been watching other people intently. He was trying to nail down exactly what it was about them, and why he was so completely comfortable with them and felt so compelled to connect. He again watched, amused, as they negotiated their way to the appropriate section of the hospital, noting that most of his fear was gone.

It was crazy just how much fear he'd been carrying around all his life. There had been tiny fears in his background thoughts for most of his life. Minuscule, insignificant thoughts that on their own were almost nothing, and almost unnoticeable, but combined, they had taken him away from the experience of really enjoying moments, of really seeing people.

Concerns about appearance, physical threats, thoughts about the future and thoughts about money. They'd piled on top of one another, clamouring for attention, drowning out quieter, freer thinking. These thoughts were now mostly gone, and he was left with a gaping, silent emptiness.

For the most part, there was silence and a constant, blissful awareness of the miracle of existence. The absence of fear allowed him the space to truly observe. He was now an observer of his own life, a version of himself driving a body around and watching everything. His wife instinctively hooked her arm through his and led him. She noticed him drift away from this world and into the state he spent much of his time.

Though he was gaining mobility and balance, he'd lost some peripheral vision on the left side. His impaired vision was only partly the reason she felt compelled to take control. He was like a small child. The world, now, was an incredible kaleidoscopic wonderland. This took his attention regularly and completely, for long moments rendering him immobile, mesmerised by its layers and brilliance. Its shininess pulled at him, distracting him from the simple task of walking through the car park.

They eventually navigated the labyrinth of the hospital and reached the waiting room for the results clinic. Families were there already, waiting for their call. They were all in a similar position. A loved one had also had an operation on their brain, and they had also waited the week or so for the results of the pathology and the success or failure of the surgery. They waited in the large room, in seats facing the same direction, like some shitty entertainment venue. They would glance at one another, almost afraid to start a conversation. Just being in that place required effort, and it was almost too much energy to engage with others. The air was heavier here. The pink walls, probably chosen by an expert to calm the patients, added a surreal thickness to the room.

He sat, quietly, taking in the space and its muffled suffering. He could feel the other patients and their families, their pain, and eventually struck up conversations, weaving gently through the hazy self-protective walls they'd erected. He wanted to help somehow. He was aware that some of those he wanted to help were in a similar position to him. He passed on the details of the meditation program that had got him through so far, noticing that he was not particularly concerned about the outcome of his surgery's result. Even now, he was sure he was going to survive for a while.

The White had said, "this is not your time."

The absence of his concerns was not only from that 'conversation'. He remembered clearly that behind everything was **The Source**, and that to experience it was sublime.

Even if he did die from this cancer, he knew that there was more, so much more to existence than even his recent awakening suggested. That feeling of boundlessness, of complete and eternal love, took all the pain from even this moment.

One by one the families were called. Emerging sometime later, sobbing, leaning on one another. Shocked and pummelled by the results, pain pushed into their faces. Their lives were forever altered by the words uttered by the men who had recently had their hands inside their bodies.

He could see the effects of this on his wife. He tried to distract her with small talk until his name was called. He smiled inwardly as he considered the amount of waiting he'd done all his life because of the alphabet. The W's were usually the last called. Under normal circumstances, waiting wasn't a big problem, but here it compounded and amplified the tension. Every second of angst was building on top of the next, crushing the breath from the people in the room and loading the air with adrenaline and fear. He sat quietly, watching all this unfold in front of him.

The large tree just outside the second-floor window moved in the wind, waving to him, almost calling him to notice it radiating life, pulsing with light. It was, like everything else now, almost insubstantial in its physical form but spectacular in its kaleidoscopic light show. Barely moving, only just breathing, he was completely aware of his connection to timeless energy. Bizarrely, other than being conscious of the suffering of the others here, he was almost unaffected by the drama being played out in this room, in this tiny corner of the cosmos.

The nurse removed the staples and returned him to his wife and the waiting room. He waited his turn to see the neurosurgeons.

Eventually, they entered a small nondescript room. It seemed strange that a space in which lives were altered in such a dramatic way was so… ordinary. They sat and moved through the niceties before moving on to results.

The cancer was malignant and it was a melanoma. It was in his lungs and what they'd taken out of his brain. The surgeons fielded their queries with the same finesse as they wielded their knives, deflecting questions for which they had no answers.

The pathology tests were done on the other side of the country and they hadn't arrived. They were waiting for some information that would define his treatment programme. He would have to return again and repeat this process in a week. It did, however, seem that his future was with oncology. Sitting quietly, he smiled through all of it. Some of his smiles stemmed from the ridiculousness of smiling in the face of this. Melanoma was not good. He had, without intervention, about nine months to live, and yet he sat, calmly watching the events like a mildly amusing TV show. He had no fear of death.

Now that he had a better idea of what he was facing, he thought about home. He wanted to go back to the other side of the country, back to his dirt, his grass, back to his children, back to his people who had stood in support and shown their love so willingly. He wanted this part of the journey to be with his crew close by. He wanted to go back and look them in the eyes and thank them for their love. They had no clue just how much their simple actions meant to him.

The surgeon brought him back into the room.

"You can't fly home."

Hearing this rocked his quietness. His mind stalled. Then, laden with processing this news, his mind slowly started ticking over, pushing aside the quietness that had pervaded previous parts of the conversation.

"You'll have to have another scan in a week to make sure that all the air from the surgery has gone. The pressure from the flight can force your brain down your spinal cord. You will need another scan, and if it's clear, you can fly home."

They returned to the car and drove mostly in silence. They wanted to go home. They wanted to be with the girls. He couldn't imagine how they were feeling. The desire to be sitting with them, talking, making family noise as only families can, was visceral. He wanted that familiar banter and hum that happened when his family was together. So many words had been written about perspective and how moments like these made it clear about what was important. It was glaringly true.

Tiny moments with loved ones are taken for granted, and yet are the most precious things that exist. He could see how money, things and status were unimportant; purely trinkets the ego liked to collect. The important things are people and planet, life, kindness and love. His kids were everything. They would have no clue how important they were to him; no clue how they had got him through this. They would never know how adoring them called him to be a better person, and how it gave him the energy to be strong. He could curl up and feel sorry for himself, but it wasn't his style. Besides, how would that serve anyone, particularly his family?

The kids were on the other side of the country. Without their parents, doing battle with all of the responsibilities of getting themselves ready for school, running the house and managing the reality of their father having cancer. He wanted to hug them, fix things, take away their fear, and yet, he knew that there was no avoiding the realities of life. There was pain, there were responsibilities, but suffering was not mandatory, even with this. He knew that their time would come, eventually, to face their own mortality. That they would experience pain.

The White had made it clear; this place is fleeting, the suffering here is fleeting, and that everyone will one day go home. His job was not to protect. It was to play and give light. It was to guide them towards ways of finding light in pain, to appreciate the gift of life, in all its shades.

They returned to the empty house. The heavy quietness allowed them both to manage this new delay in the best way they could. He watched his wife. There was no way he could reach her, nothing he could do to soften her suffering. He felt her pain, but in a way he'd never been able to before. He was strangely detached, yet full of compassion. In the past, her suffering was somehow a reflection on him. He'd made it personal. He wasn't able to make her happy. He was finally clear that she had her own path and it was hers to negotiate. All he could do was be the best he could be. He could shine as much light as possible.

***

It was cold. And late. He was drenched in sweat and his bladder dragged him from sleep. It was a strange sensation now, waking up. There was small freedom as the world formed around him. As it became more solid there was a weight that leaned on him. It arrived the moment he remembered he'd just had a tumour removed. It sat there for a bit, waiting for the machinations of his new way of thinking to dissipate the possibilities of cancer.

The thoughts of cancer and death strangely were a doorway to an incredible paradox. He was conscious of the ugliness of melanoma, yet acutely aware of his expanded view of existence because of it. The experience of facing death had made experiencing life indescribably wonderful.

This entire sequence of feelings and associated internal conversations had taken place in the moments before he had even placed his foot on the floor. The room was pitch black. He was in a bedroom in the depths of the universe. The atoms that made up his feet dropped onto the atoms that made up the uneven terracotta-tiled floor, and he shuffled through the abyss towards the toilet. He placed his hands on walls and doors, partially for safety but also to feel the solidity of things, to take in their texture, to savour the experience of them.

He felt the sweat cool on his skin. These night sweats were a relatively recent thing and had started some months before. The cancer had been doing some strange things to his body, which made sense now. The sweats were part of that. He'd never noticed the sensation of sweat cooling and drying in such detail before. It seemed all his senses were heightened, and also infused with wonder. Almost all physical experiences took him instantly to the awareness of the unfathomable series of events that led his body to be here, now.

This was closely followed by the awareness of being aware. He was conscious, mindful of the experience of being alive and mindful of being conscious of the experience of being alive. It was blissful. **The Source** was just there, at his fingertips. He smiled as this dialogue led him again to the realisation that he was, as all others were, **The Source**. That he was not separate from it. The mundane had become sublime, the realisation each time bringing him to tears of joy. What a gift.

The toilet was at the beginning and off to the right side of a hall that eventually led to the kitchen and lounge. As he felt his way up the hall with tentative steps, the lights in the distance, across the water, caught his attention. The closer he got to the end of the hall, the more the view opened up. At first, the lights of humanity sparkled and bounced off the water, but with each step closer to the windows, more pinpricks of cosmic radiation cut through the billions of miles between him and the stars. They spread out in front of him, millions of stars thrown across the blackness by **The Source**, like sprinkles flung by children across an endless black tablecloth. He sat on a stool, leaned on the bench, feeling his way through each of these movements, before finally taking in this scene completely. There seemed to be no separation between the sky and earth. The edge of the earth was barely perceptible. It seemed entirely appropriate that it should appear that way. There was no separation.

He sat in the darkness, the light of the stars and street lights across the river falling over his face and the bench in front of him. His wife was asleep, ensconced in a warm bed. He needed to cool down for a while. The phone was on the bench. He reached for it and began to write, even before he was aware of what he was doing.

Despite the speed of his clumsy one-finger typing, the words fell out:

```
"I have run through the streets of a sleeping
   city, alone, broken-hearted and exhilarated.
I've felt the sting of the rain on the beach in
 the tooth of a cyclone while holding the hand of
   my daughter, leaning into the wind, dancing.
```

I've had love, and loved from the bottom of my heart, crying from the pain and joy of it.

I have tasted mangos, had watermelon juice run down sunburnt arms, plump with the soreness from surfing till I can't. I have stood with brothers and sisters, sweating, heaving, suffering from the effort of mastering movement, quieting the voice urging rest. NO. Another kick, another punch. Just… one… more.

I have had the sharpness of guilt gnaw at my insides and the glory of releasing it when I cleaned up my crap. Felt the inexpressible joy of contribution, of giving to others just because I can. I've held the hand of my youngest baby as she wrestled with the newness of her first dance class.

I have tasted from most of the plates we are supposed to, and some of the ones we are not. Swayed to music in the dark, felt the bark of a hundred trees, the warmth of a thousand rocks.

For this, all of this and more, I am grateful. Grateful beyond words, for the pain, the joy and everything in between. Grateful to my wife. Grateful to my friends and family for being with me in this.

If I go to the light, to the stars, I go there with these words:

'Thank you for this gift, this incredible gift of life. It's been a pleasure, every little bit.

A monumental, indescribably beautiful, pleasure.
Thank you, thank you, thank you.'

I have **felt."**

Finally cooled down, he ran his hands over the texture in the walls, using them as a guide back to the blankets and the warmth.

Good coffee was something he'd enjoyed before the surgery and while, strangely, he had lost all desire for anything sweet, a good coffee was still wonderful. He and his wife were settling into a routine of waking, exploring, and then a medicinal nap, interspersed with a coffee. It was nice to just be, with no distractions, to talk in a way they hadn't for a long time. They did the small things required of them and then took time to just be together, to have meals, to have a coffee and to sit and people watch.

Tears Of Beauty

One of their trips out and about was to an art supply shop. This particular shop had sponsored him to do a demonstration here before his collapse. The whole purpose of his trip was to hold an exhibition and a series of painting demonstrations and workshops along the Coast. It had been an ambitious schedule. The exhibition was complete, but the tumour had interfered with it, and his ability to run the workshops and demos. He'd managed to shamble through some of the earlier obligations before finding himself in hospital.

Now that he was out, and alive, he wanted to see if his painting ability had been affected and if so, by how much. The paint company and art supply store people reinforced the goodness of humanity by making everything he needed available. He eventually found his way back to the house, setting himself up with a view of the river, and a place to make a mess.

His first brush strokes and movements were clumsy. He managed to make some marks just the same but felt some of the deftness of his touch had gone. The process was slower. He was ok with that because he knew these processes could be re-developed. After all, he'd learnt them once.

Because his brain was much quieter now, the machinations of his thinking were more obvious to him. Questions began to emerge.

"Where's the light coming from?"

"How do I make this mark?"

"What would happen to this shape if the light was coming from here?"

All these questions he'd asked himself unconsciously thousands of times. With this realisation, the tears came. Tears of beauty. He dropped to the floor, sobbing.

The questions were still there. That was the most important part. The physical stuff could be learned again, but the question was where all the answers were. He'd often been asked 'How do you know when a painting is finished?' And he'd never really had a clear answer before. Now he did.

"A painting is finished when the questions are all answered."

He could not have been any happier. His life long passion was still there and functioning. He looked across the river and said over and over again.

"Thank you, thank you, thank you, thank you."

The Storm

The media had built up the storm so much that even here, on the other side of the country, there was a slightly ominous air hovering over everything. There was a collection of meteorological events, which, on their own, would have been threatening. They were joining together in some monstrous superstorm that bore down on the length of the East coast.

The wind, rain and seas were all they promised to be, and people eventually set about cleaning up, after the storm had done its thing. The phone, his link to home, kept him up to date with a group of friends and others from his area who had organised to do some work at his house. He had neglected his garden for over twelve months prior to this trip. He was beginning to realise just how dysfunctional he'd been, overwhelmed by work and all the obligations he'd had. All of which would have been manageable had he not been growing a tumour.

The group were a collection of men who were close friends and acquaintances, but all were people he'd known for a long time, and who were determined to do something to help. They attacked the garden, removing trees that had fallen in the wind, removing rubbish and tidying up. On the surface, they were things that seemed practical, things that he would not be able to do for a while, if ever. They weren't just small things. They were monumental, epic things. They shovelled, carried and cut. This was everyday work that shifted stars.

His wife relayed to him the plans and the progress of their efforts. There was support that came from both sides of the country and not just from these men. He had some social media platforms, though he was unable to look at them. The responses and love were too much. It felt like the whole world had his back.

That he truly was loved.

He sat with the impact of these apparently ordinary people who did something extraordinary. They generously gave up their time and energy to help, to labour. They gave him light. They gave him hope. Their generosity brought him, all six foot and eighty plus kilos of him, to his knees. These people left him in tears, in awe, humbled and breathless.

The consequences of these simple actions were incomprehensible. They lifted and inspired. He couldn't believe that they'd done that for him. He pushed some broken words towards his wife.

"I don't deserve this."

They were met with her words, parried and absorbed.

"Yes, you do. You've helped the community, given your paintings to all sorts of causes. You helped kids, taught them karate, taught them to paint, often without pay. You've listened and helped friends and others who've needed it. This is your turn."

Understanding that he really was part of a community only highlighted how precious it was. He saw that a single soul could create a community around them; that being generous for no reason, just to help, created a space into which more generosity could appear. It was clear that there was a community that cared, and that cared about him.

It was incredible that he'd had this experience with **The Source** and so many questions were now answered. To be accepted and loved by **The Source** was understood, almost expected. A being that was pure light and love would accept and love. But to be loved and accepted in this three-dimensional world was a new form of validation and acceptance for him, and the icing on the cake.

He was now completely raw, unprotected and exposed to the world. There were no more walls, no need for him to protect himself. He had largely shed his ego. He actually was enough, flaws, imperfections and all, both here and 'there'. In this moment he was free to be who he really was, not the creature this three-dimensional solid world had imposed on him. He was liberated from his identity.

The shell had fallen away.

The News

The lounge was comfortable and modern, with lots of glass. He quite enjoyed not having to be anywhere or do anything other than rest. He was still not entirely comfortable walking around, still unsteady. Sitting quietly in the room in the mornings, taking in the warmth from the heater, was heavenly.

The television called him and he flicked on the news. He sat watching, almost dispassionately, as the list of human tragedies flew across the screen, interspersed with ads for cars that would make you the 'envy of your neighbours'. Once, he would've been angry at the hypocrisy, greed and stupidity of human behaviour. Now, he just sat quietly, slightly saddened by the unnecessary suffering.

He understood why people did what they did. He understood that the perpetrators of hideous crimes were themselves victims and in pain, unable to find a different way of being. There was as much sorrow for the perpetrators as the victims. They had no idea what damage they were causing themselves. Aware of the greater forces at play now, it wasn't for him to know the paths that others were on.

He knew nothing about anything, just that he was here to play and give light.

The screen lit with images of the Middle East. Images of men kneeling beside their knife-wielding captors. At one time, these images would have been hard for him to see without becoming deeply upset. This time, surprisingly, he felt deep sympathy for those holding the knives. Their victims were going to the light, to love, to The Source. He knew what that was like. There was no longer sorrow for those who died. While there was the deepest empathy for those who were left, there was nothing for those who went Home.

Lost in these thoughts, he watched himself process this new way of being. His thoughts drifted and he wondered. 'Why? Where will mindlessness and cruelty lead? Would humanity eventually destroy itself? And for what purpose? What could possibly be good about all this suffering?'

The White words again seeped into the entire world he occupied, in the same way they had before, immense and layered words, filling him entirely.

"The White Is Coming."

It was somehow clear that it meant that the experience of The White was coming to many. In fact, to most of humanity. He noticed there was some concern. What did that mean? Were millions going to die and go Home? Were wars, or some type of environmental collapse, going to end the lives of millions? Were his children part of that and would they suffer?

Holding these thoughts at a distance, he turned them over, taking them apart and investigating them in the light of what he now knew. The words again enveloped him.

"The White Is Coming."

His concern disappeared. There was nothing to fear. This was 'accounted for'. Millions may die, it was entirely possible. It was now clear to him that widespread death and destruction was not inevitable. What was inevitable was that The White was coming. People were 'waking up'. There were millions like him. Some who were shown in the same way he'd been. Others who knew or believed these discoveries instinctively.

Either way, people were waking up. Humanity was realising the limitations of thought patterns that were primarily about survival, about scrabbling to the top of the heap. There was little real joy or meaning in that existence. We wanted more. More bliss, more fulfillment, more love.

We wanted life.

There were millions and millions of people making that shift, and their numbers were growing every day. There would be a critical mass in the not too distant future, and more people would awaken. This was the next stage of evolution. This was where we moved beyond our animal nature, where we left cruelty, greed and reactive behaviour behind. This was coming.

The White was coming.

Going 'Home' Home

This trip to the results clinic had an entirely different flavour to the last. His wife had spent the days prior battling with the airline, trying to get a flight home. Their departure that night back to the other side of the country, back to a more familiar part of the world among their friends, and back to their children who had been struggling without their parents, all depended on this meeting. They went through the process of parking, waiting, and eventually sitting in front of the surgeons.

The tears fell even before the words had finished crossing the room to their ears.

"The scan is clear, you can fly."

They sobbed in each other's arms before turning to the doctors and thanking them between sniffles and watery smiles.

The house was packed up and they headed to the airport. Their driver was a man who'd initially been doing some work with him and had become part of the support network. His willingness to help was amazing. He was living proof that beneath everything, humanity was fundamentally good. He had gone above and beyond what would have been enough. They sat at the airport almost in disbelief that they were finally heading East.

The wheels left the runway. Flying was something he had a lot of experience with, but none of the flights meant as much as this. He wanted to be home with his girls, back with the red dirt of the New South Wales North Coast, and back with his community. To get to this point, there were hoops to jump through with the airlines. Forms had to be produced and plans made in the hope of being free to fly. He floated through these dramas watching his wife struggle with everything. He'd been unable to help her much, unable to offer any real assistance. Trying to help her made it clear to him his brain was not working the way it once had.

While he was completely at peace, his inability to process much of the logistical nightmare his wife was wrestling with, was obvious. All he could do was quietly support. He sat between two worlds. One, the peace and ease of 'knowing', and the other, watching someone he loved struggle. He wanted to download this new understanding to her, help her step free from the suffering. It was clear to him that it was possible to be with pain, but suffering with it was optional. The response or attitude to 'misfortune' determined the level of suffering.

He straddled her pain and his bliss, caught between the two, wanting to help but not able to buy into the upset of the moment. Trying to console her, he tried to let her know that his distance wasn't because he didn't care. He did, endlessly, but it was difficult for him to see much of the machinations of this crude three-dimensional place. This world, with forms and money and pain, was now so fleeting and insubstantial. The 'other place' behind, beyond, under, and eternal, made the concerns of his life almost inconsequential.

The aircraft tilted abruptly and threw itself into the star-studded sky. Five hours in the stars then back, back on the ground on his side of the country.

The surge of the engines, coupled with the quiet pop of his ears adjusting to the pressure, brought a mild concern about flying. The scans had shown the air that was in his head from the surgery had dissipated. That being said, he unconsciously put his hand to his head, feeling the wound, and feeling the sensations in his head, trying to pre-empt any problems. If there was any air in his skull, it could expand as the pressure changed and force his brain down his spinal column.

"Coning, is that what it's called?" he asked himself. "It's fine, they said it was fine to fly."

Relaxing, he took his hand from the wound, shoulders dropping. Sitting back, a small part of him watched the deeper corners of his brain, just in case.

He looked into the abyss through the aircraft window. They were hurtling through the darkened sky. Stars, clear and sharp, were unmoving and unmoved as the distance between them and home diminished. It was late. The flight had been delayed and they'd finally arrived, with his brain intact and where they were supposed to be. The hotel was the last stop before home. Sleep, a couple of hours in the car, and they'd be home.

Only a few kilometres from home, they took a detour through the town to one place in particular.

Walking along the bank, he took in the smell of the sea, listened to the waves, watched the grass blow in the wind. Every single minute aspect of the moment. He wallowed in it. He was alive, more alive than he'd ever been. The ground felt uneven under his slightly unsteady feet. It was only about three weeks since the surgery. He'd healed well. In fact, had surprised everyone by how well he'd recovered, but he could feel the difference. His normal sure-footedness had given way to a lack of confidence. Any distress he may have had about that was drowned by his excitement. Some of his friends were at the top of the bank. He couldn't wait to see them.

They were standing where they always stood, looking at the surf, fixing the world's problems, and generally tormenting each other in the way true friends do. He hadn't seen them for weeks; since he'd left for the other side of the country, since before the surgery. These were people he'd known for years. They'd surfed with him and tasted parts of his life, in the way people in small towns do with familiarity and time. They were people who had called him at the hospital, concerned for him, people who had been worried; had worked in his garden when he was incapacitated, shown their love in their men way, all backslaps and taking the piss.

He knew he loved these people. Truly, deeply loved them. Men don't cry. He had heard that many times. They did now, here. He hugged and laughed and cried and slapped. He'd never realised how much he loved his community and his town.

Eventually, this feeling waned. He was finally distracted from his friends by the ocean. This place felt like *his* bit of ocean. He had surfed there or around this place for over forty years. It had never been so beautiful.

He had, for a time, felt he would never get back here.

Walking down to the water, he stopped and squatted in the shallows, feeling the grains underfoot as his feet sank into the wet sand. A small wave rushed at him, as salty tears simultaneously rushed from him, back to the ocean.

The moment, *this* moment, had taken millions of years to create. Stars had disintegrated, spewed their collective essences into the heavens to join, to fuse into this place, now. He studied the grains and gripped them in his hand, trying to hold them. He held the fragments of stars in his hands, an almost endless sequence of events bringing them to his fingertips. His tears were without pain. They were tears of rapture. He was back, back with people he loved, in a place he loved, but now he was conscious of being able to reach through this physicality and touch **The Source**. He squatted amongst the stars and truly understood the words 'heaven on earth' to the core of his being.

After

He was back in his town. Back on his side of the country. Back with familiarity and the security that comes from being in a place for a long time. Despite all that history and familiarity, this place was now different. Same trees, same buildings.

Same, but different.

There was a hum, a fizz that permeated everything. The light he'd seen emanating from everything in Perth was here too. This light was subtle and incredibly beautiful; as if he could now see and feel life itself.

He had a sense of experiencing his home on this entirely different level, like looking at the world without any filters, allowing him to see it in a whole new way. He was very clear that this new way of seeing had been there all the time. This wasn't *actually* new; he'd just never seen it.

The humble mosquito could see the world in an entirely different way from how humans saw it. Dolphins, bats and dogs had access to seeing the world in ways we couldn't perceive or comprehend with any real understanding. He began to realise the limitations of human senses. There was a way of experiencing the world, outside of those senses. It was interesting how we assumed that if we couldn't see, feel, hear, smell, or taste it, it wasn't there.

"What if we could 'see' the world if we removed some of the filters we had?"

This led him to the next question. Why could he now 'sense' this light and this fizziness? He hadn't before the surgery. What had happened to change things?

At first, it seemed to him that the only possibility was that something in his brain had been interfered with and altered in some way. He wanted to do some research to try and find out why the world, and he, were now so different. The way the world now appeared to him, and the reactions he had to it, were almost incomprehensible.

He had tumours in his lungs, the threat of growing another in his head, and yet, he was largely in awe at the magnificence of the existence of everything, including himself. He could barely raise much concern over his life-threatening circumstances.

Trying to dissect the layers he was seeing, he found it difficult at first to pin down. It came from everything and everywhere. It was all-pervasive. It wasn't separate - he was not separate. He'd realised in Perth that he was connected somehow to everything, but now standing here in his home, thousands of kilometres from the hospital and the site of his collapse, he saw the connection.

That fizzy light connected all things, particularly life. As a result, everything was indescribably wonderful and glorious.

The epic convulsions of the stars and their energies were right there.

First Surf

He had had some concerns about his first surf. There was the uncertainty of how capable he currently was, given his balance issues. There was another more pressing concern; the question he'd been asked by one of the neurosurgeons.

"Have you had a fit yet?"

There was something about the way he'd asked that had made it seem at least one was inevitable. Thus far, he hadn't had one he was aware of. There'd been a few moments where he felt his brain almost stop, the coloured wheel spinning for a while as he processed an oversupply of information, but no seizures so far. Apparently the further he got from the surgery, the less likely it was.

It forced him to consider that if it was inevitable, would he have one in the surf? He was pretty sure that was not a good option but wasn't going to let the thought keep him out of the ocean.

Taking his longboard out of its cover, feeling its familiar lines, he walked towards the beach much more carefully than he once would have, some residual unsteadiness slowing his pace.

The board was familiar and consoling. He loved that board. This longer, bigger board would give him some time to get to his feet and hopefully be stable enough for him to stay up.

It was clear that the beach was still affected by the huge swells that had blasted the coast only a month or so before. His favourite spot to surf usually benefited from a big swell. The huge amounts of moving water tore the sand away from a reef that formed long, fun waves when the wind and swell lined up. Today, the wind was right but the swell was tiny.

Thankfully, tiny was about all he could handle. This was to be his first surf in over two months, and his first surf since the brain surgery.

He paddled out around the breaking waves and over the reef, feeling his muscles working and how much his incapacitation had weakened him. He wondered how it would all go. Could he catch a wave, could he stand, and could he stay up?

The plan was just to paddle around for a while. He convinced himself that this was all it was, a paddle. No harm in that. He knew though, that was a complete lie. If a reasonably respectable wave came along, he'd take it. The instinct and joy of riding waves were just too strong.

There were a few people out. All locals, and people he knew. He sat on his board and watched for a while, mesmerised by the water, tasting the air and basking in the day. It was clear and a bit cool, the wind offshore and a little brisk.

Eventually, a wave came and he paddled into it. The sounds of the water furrowing around him and the board, the sensations of speed, cool wind and spray, almost distracted him. He looked at the wave walling out in front of him, grabbed the rails, pushed down and jumped up. He was up. He leaned and turned the board, trimming across the face, making adjustments to avoid coming off and prolonging the ride.

He was standing. He was surfing. He was alive.

The reef flew beneath him. This tiny wave was magnificent. It eventually flattened and he leant, pushed the tail deeper into the water and turned the board back towards the ocean, before dropping back to his belly.

The momentum from the wave and a few paddles had him back off the reef and away from any breaking waves. After making sure there were no waves looming, and still on a high from the first, his head dropped and he cried. A deep, satisfying, grateful sobbing. A soft voice came through his tears.

"You right, Markus?"

It was one of his local mates. A bloke around town he'd known for years. He was older, and a surfing legend, so had mixed generally with an older crew, but as in all small towns was one of the village 'brothers'.

He looked up through salty eyes to see a wizened face.

"Yeah mate, I'm good." And he was. His tears were like liquid gold. They were tears of pure joy. They were the tears of a man who was seated at a buffet after having believed he would never eat again. "Didn't think I'd get to do that again."

More tears came, from both sets of eyes, as they lay together on their surf crafts, bobbing amongst the waves. Tears of gratitude, relief, and joy.

Settling

As he settled into his life, it became very noticeable how people responded to him.

In the hospital in Perth, he'd been provided with an end of life counsellor. After the inevitable discussion about care and death, the counsellor mentioned something that would permeate many of his conversations for a long time afterwards.

She had very casually mentioned that he would spend a large part of his time consoling others about his condition.

It proved to be true. People now did very strange things, some even crossing the road to avoid him. He understood their discomfort. In the past, he also found it difficult to talk to people who were going through similar circumstances. Fear of his own mortality had tainted his ability to really be with them. There was an unconscious distance he'd put between him and them, a void in which to avoid mentioning anything that would come too close to the reality of the person's circumstance. He could see that this was a very human, primal, survival response, and could understand.

It was his turn now.

Smiling inwardly as he watched their mental convulsions, he set about giving them the space to relax. His casual and offbeat humour usually worked, although there were occasionally some he couldn't quite soften.

Conversations would start with the throw away greeting: "Hi, how are you?"

This simple question left an interesting space. The world that it opened sometimes led to an uncomfortable moment.

Some people were easy and just leapt straight in, asking about the current status of the tumours and treatments. This made it easy. Nothing to avoid. He could update them, and pepper the conversations with a few bad and/or irreverent jokes about cancer. Their openness made it easy. He called them 'The Reals'.

The rest could be split into a few groups.

The first group would start off awkwardly, loosening up as they realised he was not freaking out. His acceptance of the possibilities of cancer gave them all some lightness and they relaxed.

The second group were in the 'No really, how are you really?' brigade. He called these people the 'No, But Reallys'. Despite his joy at being alive, a few of these people almost got headbutted.

This group seemed unable to accept his ease with the state of play. Some of these people would often repeat the question several times. They couldn't seem to understand that he was completely at peace with his diagnosis. He realised it was their fear that prevented them from hearing him and let them be. Occasionally he would respond with a cheeky, "It's okay, I wouldn't swap my life for yours". This usually settled the conversation.

The third group was different altogether. They were known as 'The Invisibles'. They would disappear completely. Some would cross the road. Some would shift awkwardly from foot to foot before making an excuse to leave. Others, despite being in his life regularly, totally evaporated. No calls, nothing. He would call some of these people to see if they were okay, some responding with 'it's all too hard to deal with'.

He understood. Some of these people had watched other friends die from cancer recently. They were traumatised. 'Not again' was unconsciously uttered.

While he was largely impervious to much of this and aware that people had their own lives and problems, he was a little disappointed. He'd considered himself quite close to some of those people.

The sick people were different. He was drawn to them now, particularly cancer people. He could see them from miles away and usually sense where they were on their journey. He could feel whether they were sad, suffering, or at peace.

It was nice to sit and really be with them. They were part of a family now. He could lighten things for them if they needed, or share cancer stories. They could laugh at things 'ordinary' people couldn't or wouldn't. It was like a slightly dark and strange but lovely club of people, united by many people's greatest fear. The big 'C'.

They would laugh about what ridiculous thing he was hoping to do with his ashes, and how they dealt with the 'No, But Reallys'. They, in turn, would fire back their crazy plans and strategies.

It wasn't funny to many outsiders, but this club was aware of the temporary nature of life and the inevitably of death and collapse. This made most of the 'ordinary' concerns and day-to-day dramas incredibly funny and inconsequential. The knowledge that everything will break down, including them, crushed the mundane worries of life.

When death was placed in front of you and deeply seen to be a natural process, it lost its power.

He'd even begun to enjoy his trips to the chemo ward. There were regulars there. People who knew. They seemed to instinctively know when to give each other space and when to engage. Usually it was banter and some jokes. While the nature of the space was confronting and a reminder of cancer, it was overall a pleasant enough place.

Other groups that drew his attention were children, the elderly and the sick. They were closer to **The Source**.

These people called him to be a kinder version of himself. He walked away from those interactions with a full heart.

Sometimes, he struggled. At times, it was difficult to be as kind and loving to people who were healthy and wasting their precious, statistically allotted eighty-odd years destroying the planet for status. Or missing out on life because of fear of an imagined future.

This was the gift of his cancer and his experience. His time was precious. He wanted to spend as much time as he could, playing and giving light.

2018

Over a year and a half since the surgery, and he has recovered well. Back surfing and painting, he's doing most things he did before May 23rd, 2016. He feels incredibly lucky to have escaped the possible consequences of brain surgery. It's a testament to great doctors and a government funded medical system. It saved his life to this point.

Stage 4 Metastatic Melanoma in the brain and lungs was historically difficult to survive, and usually, death came very quick.

There have been some consequences from having someone stick their hands inside his head. He has some processing issues when things get emotional, and occasionally gets overwhelmed when there is a lot going on. But on the whole, he's sort of back to normal, although most of his friends would argue he was never that to begin with.

Tomorrow he has his last dose of radiation, and in two months he has scans to see the results. One of the tumours in his lungs had begun to misbehave and needed a dose of radiation to pull it into line. Despite this, the truth is that he doesn't give too much time to the tumours, or the possibilities of them. It's not to say he doesn't think of them sometimes, or that he is in denial of his 'cancer dance'. He just refuses to suffer psychologically with them.

***

From the writings on his phone:

Radiation

The machine is impersonal but no less ominous. It squats in the centre of the efficient and sterile room, humming imperceptibly… waiting.

The room is silent, cool.

Everyone has left.

This room is dangerous… for them.

I can't move in this room. My mind says tomb. I am strapped, clamped and incapable of scratching the itch that starts the moment I am immobile.

The machine waits, holding the energies of the cosmos, ready to pour them into this fragile sack of skin and bone and flesh.

This machine could be, perhaps should be, terrifying… but it's not.

It is miraculous.
It constrains and directs the life force of the stars. It holds a flicker of the building blocks of the universe in its depths.
We puny humans play with energy like children, naive and ignorant. We blindly brush against the nectar of 'The All'.

This toy holds a taste of the blood of stars.

> It is a morsel from the All That Is.
>
> I weep in this machine.
> Not from fear or pain. I weep because I am
> bathed in the source of All.
> All is energy.
> All is Source.
> All is.
> I Am.

He is not 'fighting' cancer. Cancer can't stand in the wind and feel the rain on its cheeks; it can't feel the surge of a wave pick you up and have it throw you at the land. It can't feel the joy of an act of kindness, and it can't look into the eyes of its children and see how wonderful they are.

He can. He can do all these things and so much more. He can feel the hum of life in his body. He's not fighting cancer. He's outliving it. Whether it takes his body or not, he's going to out*live* it.

That pile of words had been thrown into people's ears quite flippantly over the last eighteen months, but he knows that statement is layered, covering in some profound ways his new way of being. He is more at peace than he has ever been, more patient than he has ever been, and has fewer concerns than ever. There are moments of exquisite bliss where he is moved to tears by the miraculous beauty of life. The experience is otherworldly and rapturous. He had to learn to manage that. Having a grown man standing in a park weeping at the beauty of a tree is difficult to explain.

His brain is gloriously quiet and (for the most part) he is able to see thoughts formulating and is able to stop them before they fall out of his head and cause damage. Seeing people in an entirely different way now allows him to both relate to them and hear them in a much deeper and profound way.

Deeply in love with kindness, he laughs a lot, and laughs at the machinations of his 'human' brain. He's not sure about yours, but his is hysterical. He is, largely, exactly who he wants to be.

At peace with the world, he is also at peace with himself. Given the circumstances, this is a bit of a surprise, at least to him anyway.

The dialogue he had with **The Source** and the word 'Communicator' now comes to mind. In the instant these words were spoken to him, he knew he had to share the experience and the lessons from it. Curiously, many people who have had experiences like this have felt compelled to do the same.

Epilogue - 2020
(strap in, it's long)

Fast forward three years. Here I am sitting in my studio, and apparently, after my last tests, there's no evidence of disease. What a ride.

What. A. Ride.

In the time since my diagnosis, I've sat back and tried to work out or make sense of the whole experience, and to somehow distill it. It was a time in which my life was somehow 'smeared'. Time stood still, and yet events seemed to merge, becoming one amorphous blob - almost as though everything occurred all at once. It's made the experience challenging to articulate.

So, here goes.

In the time since the diagnosis of the tumours, I've made some interesting discoveries. Despite my excitement about them (not the tumours), they aren't new discoveries. All the reading I've done to try and explain the experiences around my surgery led me to understand that this path is very well worn. You can change a few names and a few circumstances, but the concepts seem to span our collective time on the planet and parallel many different philosophies and ideas about the experience of being alive.

So, the following is my ignorant but enthusiastic effort to both document and understand what I believe happened to me and why. We'll start with a big one.

Fear.

A funny thing happened to me while negotiating the trauma around the discovery of my illness. There was a surge of fear that I could almost smell and taste.

It was like someone sitting on my chest.

It was a really interesting opportunity to look at fear. I'm not going to pretend it was pleasant, but sitting face to face with it took me through to another understanding of fear, which was easier to experience. I also realised just how much of my life was tainted by fear.

While I thought I was living on a path that was slightly outside of that, there was still fear in the background. It wasn't the 'big' fears either that were so dangerous. It seems quite logical to be scared if a bus is bearing down on you. That fear is easier to see and usually only lasts for a short period of time.

The really dangerous fears, for me, were the small ones. I can't say how many times I've said in my life, "I don't care what anyone thinks", but the truth is - I did. Those tiny little concerns about other people's opinions, other people's judgements, fitting into societal ideals and social expectations were constantly running in the background. These are the fears that I now know to be the hardest to see, but the ones that sneak in and diminish the possibilities of joy. They were the ones that took your attention.

They took you away from the sunset, from the look on children's faces, from the light on the leaves. Those tiny little fears in the background were insidious and they sucked the juicy glorious marrow out of life.

It seems to me that fear is a necessary tool for survival, but I was unable to separate the 'real' fears from the imagined ones. It seems much clearer now that I have truly faced the ultimate fear. I can truthfully say that facing my death in a very honest way has probably been one of the most liberating things that's ever happened to me. I can now say, "I don't mind what anyone thinks", and actually mean it (...most of the time).

For me, facing my death has put all my other inconsequential fears into perspective. I don't seem to sweat the small stuff any more. I'm not keen on the transition from being alive to being dead, especially if it's drawn out and painful, however, I'm definitely not afraid of being 'dead'.

If you'd asked me how I was going to deal with a cancer diagnosis before the tumours, I would have told you I would be terrified; and I had been.

The discovery of the melanoma on my back on my fiftieth birthday was the catalyst for the fear to really make itself known.

It changed me.

The surgery that followed, the lymph nodes taken and the medical stuff that went along with that, led me to feel real and genuine, chest crushing, take your breath away, fear. I would regularly wake in a cold sweat, with the taste of adrenaline in my throat, and a bony metaphorical fist pushing into my chest.

I would try to escape the possibilities by being busy, losing myself in work and distancing myself from my family, in some strange effort to protect them if the thing had got away. I watched my Dad die of cancer and I was scared.

I struggled to manage that for a while, but as time went on, I relaxed about it a little, completely unaware that some cells had escaped the doctor's efforts to contain them. And was obviously and gradually descending into the nightmare of the reality-warping brain tumour and tumours in my lungs.

The tumour had been hiding in my brain, growing and pushing my personality around more and more as time went on. The changes were so gradual that I didn't suspect anything.

That fear came rushing back in a big way in the days following my collapse in 2016. It was in that place of fear and extreme emotional pain that I had the first of the three experiences.

When you exercise, there comes a point where the weights that you lifted before seem to become lighter as you become stronger. Perhaps fear is a little like this. Facing the greatest fear makes it easier to navigate the smaller ones.

Perhaps one of the greatest fears you can face is your own end. Your fear of the end of 'you' is a completely understandable response. We need that fear to survive. For me, that moment of no longer hiding, of standing looking at my death without anywhere to hide, eventually became indescribably liberating.

Nearly all other fears, in comparison, seemed tiny.

Living With The Light - Cancer And Fear

Cancer has been a fear of mine since my teens, and probably the biggest one. As a teen, I watched one of my mates traverse a difficult path through leukaemia, and it really scared me. I couldn't understand why, and how, a perfectly healthy person's body would just turn on them and drag them through so much pain.

As life went on, there were the inevitable brushes with others who danced with cancer and very few that survived.

My Dad, who I was sure was invincible, and who was one of the strongest people I knew, died after a long wrangle with lung cancer. He was stoic to the last, but even he wasn't able to hide his pain and suffering. It didn't help me that cancer had been his greatest fear also. His death probably cemented my fear more than anything else.

All of that fear was a background track that played behind the scenes for most of my life, but mostly far enough behind to go largely unnoticed. After the collapse in Perth, the words the lovely Irish doctor said to me in the hospital on that life-changing night, gouged deep into my memories.

"You seem like a straight-shooting kind of guy. There is no easy way to say this, so I'm just going to give it to you straight. You have a mass in your brain and some lesions in your lungs. Try not to worry, it might not be cancer."

All my nightmares and fears around cancer came out of my brain, coalesced, compressed and dropped all ten tonnes straight onto my chest. I can honestly say I've never felt a sensation like it. I'm sure I could taste the adrenaline. I definitely could feel my jaw clench and the skin up my back, and at the back and sides of my neck, tighten.

Then of course there was the hippo that dropped firmly onto my ribs, squeezing the air from my lungs and pushing against every effort to breathe. This was next level fear, and something I'd rarely experienced in that way.

After what seemed like endless hours of mental writhing, to the point of exhaustion, I remembered that I had a meditation program on my phone and, after a supreme effort of will, retreated into it. There, I found the courage to really, really look at cancer from a place free from my stories about it and its horrors.

As an aside, 'courage' isn't really the right word.

I went to a space where I could observe my newly discovered cancer, dispassionately, unattached, and somehow separate myself from it. I'd realised that facing this was something I couldn't escape. I had to stand and take it head-on.

Even in that early stage, the meditation program, and the realisations that came with it, helped me to watch the process from outside. It gave me the space to really look at the reality of my fear.

In the depths of this process, I discovered myself smiling at the melanoma. I distinctly remember being shocked at hearing myself saying to the melanoma, "you sneaky, sneaky, little bugger!", completely surprised at my admiration for it and its ability to survive.

From this new place of admiration, I was able to look closer. This was different.

I was lying in a hospital bed, looking at my greatest fear the same way I'd looked at a snake I'd picked up as a kid. Of course, there was some trepidation, but it was overcome by curiosity. Its danger was part of the attraction.

After turning it around and looking at it from as many angles as I could, I came to the conclusion that it was merely alive in some way, as I am, and trying to survive, as I was.

Cancer seemed to me to simply be a mutation; and so am I.

My body is a result of tiny mutations over millions of years. There have may have been millions of alterations in DNA that were successful at some point, were kept, and led me to be alive, here, now. In some ways, I found myself grateful for the fact that my body could have cancer. It seemed to me to be a very similar process that had my body existing at all.

Cancer was becoming harder to dislike and harder to fear. It now seemed that hating cancer was like hating your legs, or your epiglottis. What a turnaround. Now, it seemed curious to me that cancer had such a bad wrap.

Very few deaths were pretty, most involved pain, and only a few of us drop off quietly and peacefully in our sleep. So why the fear of cancer?

Was it the lingering and disintegration that was so distasteful, or was it that loved ones would have to witness and perhaps suffer through it also? It now occurred to me that perhaps cancer could be seen as a better death than a more sudden one.

Without diminishing the obvious things that come from dying slowly, there are some upsides.

There is the possibility of cleaning up your crap. As we go through life, we inevitably upset people and have conflicts. An opportunity to prepare for death is an opportunity to, perhaps, clean up those relationships. The bonus is if you survive it, you'll have more friends.

There's also the possibility of seeing and allowing your community to contribute to you. Something we rarely do.

These opportunities to clean things up are a gift to your loved ones and probably conversations that wouldn't have been had otherwise. We can sometimes be pretty stingy with our willingness to release people from our trail of carnage. This time we have to clean things up means we could die having liberated our loved ones from confusion, or a lack of clarity about our love for them.

I can honestly say that the **Love** word pops into my conversations hundreds of times more now than it ever has, and my 'cleaning up' has left me lighter and freer than I've ever been.

After negotiating this unexpected newfound admiration of cancer and some of its more positive aspects, I found myself more accepting of the place I was in. The nightmarish thoughts and fears were softened, and the hippo that had been sitting on my chest was now a large mangy dog that was almost but not quite cuddly.

There was still, however, a future to consider; a future that was heavy with the possibility of dealing with a slow and untidy death.

Cancer And People

A funny thing happened when I entered the new world, the world in which I had cancer. My relationships with people shifted completely.

Generally, everyone was very gentle and considerate. Many people were this way because they assumed I was going to die.

Imagine if we treated everyone as though they were going to die, as though they had a terminal illness. Would we be kinder, more compassionate, and patient? It certainly seemed that way to me.

How funny though, that we are that way when someone announces a terminal illness. The fact is that we're all living with a terminal illness called *Life*! We are in the delusion that someone with an illness somehow deserves more patience and kindness than the rest of us, who are in truth, in the same boat. We live with the fear and reality of death but the delusion that it won't happen to us. So we are cavalier with our time, and often lazy with our relationships and expressions of love.

When you have cancer, people come out of the woodwork with all sorts of great ideas about how you can cure your cancer. They are very well-meaning most of the time, but some of them are very intense and **very** determined that you embrace their particular cure.

Sorry, but it's not always helpful.

This can often take on extremes. I even had people suggest to me that I don't care about my children, or that I don't want to live, because I didn't take their suggestions.

The cancer patient is getting their head around the diagnosis, trying to understand what it means for them, what it means for their family, and how and if they should change their lives. There are so many opinions out there, and so many people expressing them, that it can be completely overwhelming. If anyone were to ask my advice about this, I would suggest that gently offering counsel *when it's asked for* is probably the best course of action.

Just let people know that you've got their back.

Something that became obvious to me after my diagnosis was other people's expectations that I 'fight' cancer. There seems to be a lot of attention given to the idea of fighting cancer.

"This is the fight of your life."

"He/she died after a long fight with cancer."

I chose an entirely different path. It's not for everyone, I understand. For me, cancer is natural. It's a part of life. Evolution is based on the premise of mutation. To fight against the inevitable breakdown or changes in your body seems pointless.

The entire universe is built on expansion and contraction, growth and decay, birth and death. Galaxies are built that way. Why would this tiny sack of bacteria my parents called 'Mark' be any different?

To me, it seems that there cannot be creation without destruction. Without life, there cannot be death. No death, no life. To resist death is to resist our precious lives. Our fears about survival squash the incredible magnificence of our existence.

Prior to my diagnosis, I was terrified of cancer. Now, I see it as part of existence, a miracle amongst miracles. My cancer was miraculous, part of the process of creation.

So, I chose not to fight. I chose to live. To really *live*.

I chose to give cancer no energy at all. Cancer can't stand in the rain. Cancer can't look into the eyes of people that it loves, and it can't swim and feel the wind.

I can. I can breathe. I can smell. I can touch.

I can stand next to my family, my children, and love them.

Cancer can't do any of those things.

If cancer destroyed my body, then good luck to it. I refused to allow it to take my joy of living. It may eventually take my life, but I am still going to outlive it just the same. Cancer can exist, but it can't really *live*.

I can choose to be fully *alive*.

This experience of life, billions of years in the creation, billions of years of cosmic soup and stars pulsing, radiation cracking across aeons to create… **Me**… here… now.

What a gift. What a monumental, epic gift. To be part of creation.

Cancer or not. I get to breathe.

I get to *live*…

What a fucking ***gift***.

Death

My newfound ability to look at this threat from a place that wasn't fraught with emotion allowed me to start clearly considering my personal experience with death. I touched on this in the early part of the book.

As is natural, my fear around death was justifiable from a societal and personal context, but I'd taken myself out of that perspective for a while and found peace, even in the face of it. It became clear to me how insane it is to psychologically resist death when it is absolutely inevitable, and that millions of humans over tens of thousands of years have fallen off their perches in various and often completely unpredictable ways.

How crazy. How had I maintained a fear of something as inevitable as a sunrise?

My death, if it was from this melanoma, was natural just the same. It would have been meant to be; as natural as a flower withering, as normal as a fish dying in the mouth of a shark, as commonplace as a star exploding.

With these realisations, more weight came off my chest. My death was as normal, as insignificant, as monumental, as the death of a galaxy. Me dying connected me to the universal play of energies pulsing, shifting and ultimately being reborn. With my life came death.

With my death, comes life.

My body was not separate. It was part of the universe, and the universe would not be the universe without this tiny little sack of bacteria and all its chemicals and elements.

So, my body would end. I got that. I could put that concern aside. I could actually enjoy the idea of my body being reused, of being part of something much bigger. I could even enjoy the idea of my atoms being spread amongst the stars when our planet dies, as it quite naturally and inevitably will. I was in fact stardust originally, and thoughts of returning to the stars were quite lovely.

So what was I worried about? What was it about death that concerned me?

Surrender

It seems to me that 'I' had surrendered, and I had surrendered utterly, absolutely and completely, to the idea of dying.

The concept of surrender was something I'd heard about vaguely in a spiritual context. It was something that was brushed against in the course of a conversation, touched on in personal development books, or perhaps a television show about spirituality. The potentials of surrendering were hinted at, but never enough to inspire me to investigate the idea more deeply.

To be totally honest, I'm not sure it would have been doable were my possible death not being rammed down my throat. It seems simple enough in theory, but the actual practice of surrender that facilitates a profound transformation is a little more challenging.

The surrender must be completely absolute.

All attachments to any outcomes, any stories about yourself, your life - you - in any way shape or form (even giving up any idea of any benefits from having surrendered) must be released.

For me, giving up everything, gave me everything.

Acceptance

Another spin on surrender, it seems to me, is total acceptance of what is, whatever it is. Not an easy thing to do, but it was the place that my tumours led me to, and the place that helped me live outside 'Mark'.

Who Am "I"?

An organism has a drive to survive. And sometimes, constructing an identity is a useful tool to keep it alive. An organism's awareness of itself gives it another reason to protect itself beyond just eating and procreating. The desire to survive is strengthened.

There was this moment in the hospital bed. Lying there, I was conscious of the consequences and probable outcome of Stage 4 metastatic melanoma in the brain and lungs. I was staring at the ceiling, trying to process this new reality.

I'd always been a very physical person. Shoulder charging my mates, surfing, karate, climbing trees. You name it, I was into it. Even my painting was physical. Big canvases, big movements, running around like an overenthusiastic labrador. I came face to face with the possibility that the ceiling above me was my new reality.

This was a future with machines, hospital smells, drugs, and pain. I couldn't rely on my physicality anymore. In fact, without it, who was I? This was the big question.

Everything I believed about myself was somehow woven through my physical existence. My expressions of love, my experience of life - everything was tactile and physical. What was my life without that?

There was an incredible moment at which I became very clear that 'I' was a construction. Everything I thought I had ever been was a story.

'I' was a story I'd made up.

When I was first born, I wasn't fully formed. 'Me' was something I developed. The story I made around that was also developed.

Mark Waller was an illusion.

The discovery, while not entirely new (I had brushed up against these concepts several times in my life) this time, was monumental. It was no longer a 'concept'. It was an actuality. I was actually experiencing the insubstantiality of me.

On the surface, that seems quite terrifying. We think that much of our fear is around death. And, that 'death' is represented by the end of our body, the giant sac of bacteria we walk around in.

We unconsciously assume that the death of our body is the death that we fear. It seems to me that the real fear was the death of my identity, and the death of my ego. It became glaringly clear that ego and identity are mere constructs we create in order to keep the sac of bacteria alive. The death of ego and identity, and the death of the body, are interwoven by us, but they don't necessarily have to be.

I now understood why it was so important in the past for me to be 'right'. I wasn't fighting to defend my opinions, I was fighting to consolidate my identity - to protect it. And to, therefore, 'survive'.

In the moment of releasing attachment to my ego, or any attachment to who 'I' had been, a glorious space opened up. To call that state sublime is completely inadequate.

There are no words to describe that space. None that come close, at least. It became indescribably apparent just how limiting my ego and my identity was to my experience of life.

They are a framework within which I lived. A framework that was constructed, ultimately an illusion, and ultimately a cage.

Play, Give Light, and....

Up until my surgery, I'd been 'busy'. There were always things to do, money to earn, jobs to do, obligations, responsibilities, etc; and life was quite complicated, despite my best efforts to keep it simple.

One of the gifts of my cancer is that I realised how much of that complication was completely unnecessary. Life is actually very simple.

It was 'shown' to me that there's really very little we need to do to enjoy the experience of living. Once we remove immediate survival needs from the equation, perhaps all there is to do is to play, and give light.

By play, I mean dance. Laugh. Enjoy. Cry. Feel. Embrace all of the nuance and the experiences of being *alive*. If you can find a job where you can play - fantastic.

By giving light, I mean kindness. Small acts of contribution and connection to people and the planet, for no reason.

Kindness for me is truly one of the most beautiful things. It doesn't matter how long I spend in front of a canvas, how long I spend practising my craft. Nothing I ever create in that context will even come close to the absolute beauty of a simple act of kindness. It's one of the few things we can give away almost endlessly without being diminished. In fact, being kind selflessly empowers and fulfils us.

Playing and giving light is not necessary for survival. They transcend our basic survival needs and can also transcend our ego and identity. We don't need to play, and we don't need to be kind, to survive.

When we do these things, we are taking ourselves out of a 'survival' way of thinking, and are more able to 'be' in the moment. There is no future to worry about, and no past to concern ourselves with. Just simply being in the world, being content with what is.

Because when we're genuinely playing and giving light, we truly are being present.

I discovered that focussing on playing and giving light changed the way I was in the world. It seems to me that there is another aspect to being alive that we can add to those other two concepts though, that will really transform our human experience.

Being Aware Of The Miraculousness Of Our Existence

Curiously, around the time of my brain surgery (thank you Stephen Hawking), I became incredibly conscious of the almost impossible chain of events that have occurred in order for me to breathe, write this, or indeed have a brain tumour.

Stars were formed from gases, pushed and pulled by radiation - atoms crushed, elements created, planets assembled - and from **_all_** of that, chemical and cosmic convolutions over 13.8 billion years (at time of publishing, lol) I get to breathe in, and breathe out.

It's crazy. Someone worked out that the odds of humans existing was ten trillion to one.

I'm wondering what the odds of each of us as individuals existing is?

It really is mind-boggling. We are all miracles. Every one of us. We walk on dead stars. We are made of dead stars. This planet is a miracle. Everything we touch and do is miraculous.

I tend to do things much more slowly these days. In the background, there seems to be a reminder of just how wondrous our lives are.

Every footstep, every breath.

A Future

I truly believe that the next step in human evolution is not physical. It is allowing ourselves to access so many more of the 'apps' our brains contain by releasing the restrictions of ego and identity. It truly is like having a modern mobile phone and only using it to text.

When I came to that 'place' and discovered 'Mark Waller' didn't really exist, I was liberated from all the things that I thought Mark Waller had to do. Should do. How he should be. And how he shouldn't be.

I was free to just *be*.

Nothing to do, nowhere to go, no one to be.

I've heard these words before. But the reality of truly experiencing their meaning is really difficult to describe. But here goes.

Imagine, if you can, a space in which *you* are enough.

Perfect.

Loved.

Forgiven.

Connected.

Endless.

These words have meanings far bigger than the words themselves. We come to this conversation with a limited understanding of the universe, and the world we live in, and with limited brain functions. Each of these words can be tasted in some small way. But imagine if these feelings were amplified immeasurably, and woven through every human experience you had.

That is the best way I can explain the state I was in, in the months after my surgery, and to a lesser degree now. I was at peace. I was unafraid. And I truly loved everyone.

I mention this for a few reasons. The first one is that I believe this experience is possible for everyone and is just beneath the surface. And secondly, having lived now for five years since the surgery, I have watched my ego attempt to re-assert itself. In doing so, I've also watched my level of suffering increase, as the ego attempted to re-establish itself; and decrease as I disentangled myself from it.

It seems to me that this could be a part of the process of humanity evolving. I feel as though I saw the process of creation of self, and saw it for what it is; purely a clumsy tool to survive.

It seems to me that uncovering this mechanism, and being free to choose to use it, or alternatively choose to live free from its bias in any given moment, is the key to ending much of our suffering.

On a final note… I wrote a lot after the surgery. Some stuff for this book, and other stuff - just mind farts that sat inside, poking me till I set them free. I'm being flippant of course. Many of these brain farts seem to me to be quite useful, and dare I say it, a bit profound.

Some of these have been strewn throughout the book, and here's another:

Gratitude

At first, I thought part of my job was to help people learn to paint. Fairly simple, at least on the surface. Of course, playing with my own artistic indulgences was part of that, as well as being a personal mission. I can't *not* paint.

The compulsion to push coloured goo around on canvas has been one of my greatest joys. I have spent countless hours observing, scratching, pushing paint, playing with colour, making marks, telling stories with a paintbrush, making the diminutive epic (at least attempting to), and all to try and make some understanding of my world, how it works, and my place in it.

All that effort would lead to a place I was relatively happy with, and a place that seemed to suit my usually positive and slightly idealistic view of the world. While I turned over stuff in the process of investigating, I still felt quite happy with my scratching around at 'the truth'.

Out of left field came what would at first appear to be terrible adversity. A shock in the middle of a big career experience.

I was excited about the show in Western Australia. I had produced some really nice paintings. Pictures that I felt had done some small justice to my experience of WA. Epic and raw imagery were counterbalanced by delicate nuances of colour and light and then placed against the edge of the world.

Divine.

The show was called 'Time and Space' (ironically enough). I was excited about sharing my visions of Western Australia with the people there. It seemed as though I felt the soul of the place in some way. I had no clue that the show was the culmination of a series of events that would change my life forever.

My entire understanding of my universe shifted.

The most incredible things happened to me there. I've been on a journey that has been terrifying, exhilarating, life-changing, and profoundly spiritual.

My world was thrown on its ear. BAM. Plans, dreams, goals; almost everything I considered part of my path was left wafting and uncertain. My reality, my future, became amorphous tendrils.

Crazily, the truth is that this is hysterical. It is in some ways ridiculously funny. I understand how that may sound, but perhaps the humour in this is now obvious to you (after reading).

We base our goals and life plans around a certain understanding of the world. When that understanding is altered - in fact, when *possibility* itself is altered, and not just altered but expanded exponentially in all directions - the 'tragedy' that may seem obvious can actually be a beautiful gift.

Since this event, I have realised that my job isn't necessarily about teaching people to paint. Don't get me wrong, I will still paint for as long as I can, and will still share all of my discoveries; I can't *not*. The act of making paintings is both too compelling for me to ignore, and I am too much of an oversharer to not share.

The fact is that we live amidst miracles around us, in us, because of us. We are part of something immense, and not separate, not alone.

The light that reflects from objects… the tiniest of creatures that go about their everyday jobs (for them) of running the world. We humans are far too interested in our lives to notice these things, and other millions of treasures. Truth be told, given the world we've built ourselves, it's very difficult to.

I guess the question has to be: Does this 'blindness' serve us?

Does it make our lives richer? Sweeter? I can't help feeling that it doesn't.

It somehow appears to me that our ability to see these things can have a profound impact on our levels of happiness. So why? Why is it that the purchase of a new thing can make us feel good, somehow elevate us for a while, temporarily give us status, sex appeal, comfort, safety and all the other marketing blather?

And yet observing something, and I mean **really** looking at something 'mundane', in immense detail, for a period of time, can take us to a far more profound and fulfilling state of mind. Take the ocean for example.

Every surfer knows to look for the details. When a particular swell comes from the right side of a storm in the right place, for the right amount of time, and the weather forces the air off the land and out to sea, again in the right direction, the waves behave a certain way.

The lip feathers and fragments as the wind blows into it. We know there is the potential for 'that wave'. Everything has aligned to allow a moment of sheer exhilaration when the elements conspire with myriad other factors to throw you along its face.

You travel at the whim of this lump of water and are able to control that movement (or not) for a few brief seconds. At some point the perfect opportunity for you to attempt a manoeuvre presents itself. You are faced with that delicious moment of putting everything together perfectly, generating a sense of satisfaction, or the relief of not coming unstuck so the ocean can give you a beating. A moment of glory or derision at the hands of your mates. Water people know the majesty of those moments.

As intense as they are, they're not exactly the way of looking at the world that I'm talking about. The joy and excitement in those moments, while incredible, exciting and beautiful, are in some small way a distraction from what is really going on.

Please don't misunderstand. I'm not diminishing the experience of challenging yourself against the elements, of exploring the abilities of the gift of movement; of judgment, of savouring adrenaline, of dancing with some risk. They should be experienced, embraced, adored and felt. A life without moments like these seems to me less rich, but these moments are still not what I am talking about. They are often not the moments that have us truly 'awakened'. They are a superficial experience of something much more profound.

When I think about it, it's not only the moment itself that I'm talking about at all.

There is something behind the moment itself, something less obvious, something going on within us. There is something profound but often forgotten, overlooked, or discovered in those fleeting moments, but never really experienced at a truly deep level.

This thing is **Gratitude**.

I have come to know gratitude. True, deep, universe-sized gratitude.

Not the tiny one that appears whenever I acknowledge some everyday fortune or action. And not the one that occurs when I catch a great wave.

I'm talking about profound and deep gratitude for the monumental gift that has been my life. Gratitude so profound that I sit here weeping with happiness for all the times I was able to laugh and cry, with and without my friends and my family. To savour the looks in their eyes, the warmth of their skin and every tiny nuance of each of them.

They walk among miracles.

They create miracles.

They *are* miracles.

The cosmic soup somehow coalesced into them in all their glory, full of subtlety, full of life, full of intricacies, full of love.

How incredible is this gift? Stars exploded, imploded, vaporised over immeasurable time and somehow, out of that, I got to rock my child to sleep and feel the wind on my skin.

This gratitude now extends to each remembered breath; even profound gratitude for the experience of kicking my toe. I know how that sounds, but there it is.

How did this happen? Does it matter? It just did, and it's glorious. I am monumentally, epically **grateful**.

Perhaps the source of true fulfilment and happiness can be in tiny moments, in the tiniest of insignificant moments, infused with all the gratitude for your life you can muster. Perhaps my job is not just about teaching people to paint. Perhaps my job is to document and immerse myself in gratitude. Perhaps that is where I truly discover my life.

Maybe deep gratitude is where we finally, truly *awaken*.

End Note

If you've come this far, there's something I'm just going to lay out.

I am absolutely sure of one thing. Consciousness does not begin and end with you. When your body is long gone, and your identity has gone with it, consciousness will remain. We limit our consciousness by believing it is the body and/or identity.

It is beyond either of them.

In fact, because of my experiences, I truly believe that consciousness is endless, and when experienced without the pollution of physicality and constructed identity, rapturously exquisite.

Heaven on earth is entirely possible.

Acknowledgments

In no particular order, I'd like to thank my wife Nicole (strap yourself in, Nicolara! What a ride). It hasn't been easy for you, dealing with all of this. Thank you. I love you.

My family, my beautiful girls, Jasmine and Emily, my son Samuel, my Mum Val, and brother Simon and sisters Caro and Madeleine. Thank you all.

Frankie Sharman, who's had my back ever since I met her. Then to my friends who are miracles, every one of them. Mick 'Spider' Heesom, Andy, Shane, Bern, Deana, Big Pete (thanks for the last minute advice mate, you're a legend), Bretto (Rest In Peace my friend), Ali Telfer, Jenny 'Mudbridge' Leembruggen, Kylie 'Chuckles McGoo' McGuire, Emma Freeman, Kramer, Robot, Pete and Berenice Roberts, Renee Murdoch (I will never forget that photo), the Lennox Arts Collective members who have always had my back; Julian Jett, Christine Read, Jen Banks, Narelle Bretherton, thanks for everything. The indomitable, irrepressible Graeme Stevenson.

There are so, so many people to thank that lifted me up, helped my family, helped with the logistics of life in the aftermath, and contributed hugely. Thank you. I'm sorry if I'm forgetting anyone. I have had a brain tumour you know. I will milk that for as long as possible.

It's All About The Light

I apologise to those who've been worn out by this already after only six years.

To the loveable but insane filmmaker, Jim Stevens, who happened to be around for most of my life. Thanks for filming it all. That's one helluva home movie (love ya guts Jimmy).

All the workshop participants at that time in 2016, thanks for your patience while we sorted out the refunds. Thank you to everyone who donated to my gofundme campaign at that time; this made a huge difference to me and my business. Thanks to everyone who supported my business on Youtube and through the website with emails, comments and purchases.

Thank you to the staff at our Chroma Australia family, especially Jim Cobb and Racquel Redmond. Thanks to Jackson's Art Supplies for their generosity and support.

Thanks to my Perth crew who went above and beyond, particularly Tracey Routledge, David Woodley and Summers Gallery, Ian 'Shedsy' Shedley and Kirsty Routledge, for your generosity and kindness. All the talented doctors, nurses and staff at Fiona Stanley and Sir Charles Gardiner hospitals. The staff at the coffee shop in Fremantle. You won't remember, but I do.

My Ballina treatment crew, oncology nurse Chris Liebke, all the staff at Lismore Base and Ballina Hospitals. Nerds who made groundbreaking drugs. I'm alive because of you. You all rock.

My dog Lexi, and my chickens. I love you all.

www.ingramcontent.com/pod-product-compliance
Lightning Source LLC
Chambersburg PA
CBHW070301230426
43664CB00014B/2605

"PRIVATE INVITATION"
BY
JAVON "CHIEF NETWORK" BATES

Copyrighted 2015
ALL RIGHTS RESERVED
Published by: Dreamer Publishing/Tomahawk Entertainment Group
Written by: Javon Bates
Featuring Illustrations by: Anthony Phillips Jr.

About the author:

Javon "Chief Network" Bates is a visionary who lives in Cleveland, Ohio. Like any diamond in the rough, he has many facets to him that embody the ultimate entrepreneur. Javon has carved out a niche in the music industry, publishing industry as well as the fragrance industry. As a writer, he has created personal memoirs of struggles in the urban community and collaborated with fellow writers Bruce Ballard and Anthony D. Phillips Jr. to enhance the movement.

He doesn't only stop at poetry to reach his audience, by finding other artists much like him lyrically gifted and driven to succeed it only made sense for him to create his own entertainment group of radio, T.V., music, publishing, comedy, movies and fashion. Marrying lyrics to original creative beats his music can only be described as musical bliss and sheer perfection! People are now saying this multi-faceted mogul shares his passion through whatever he touches and above all his success comes from his relentless motivation to succeed and see others succeed with him on his journey through life.

I dedicate this book to Monique Williams. We have been through a lot but at the end we will be together for eternity. I love to give a special thanks to my kids, my team and my fans. Much love to you all and thank you for your support always.

About the book

In this 3rd installment by Javon "Chief Network" Bates he releases his best work so far. In this edition he touches the surface of the hearts and souls of the reader. He expresses a deeper interaction with your vision, imagination and reality. He has some touching personal stories that will be expressed throughout the book. Some of the poems are private moments and that's why this is your "Private Invitation" inside the mind, body and soul of the author.

PRIVATE INVITATION

- Private Invitation
- Lifetime Engagement
- The Cure
- The Vision
- Listen
- My Proposal
- Resurrection
- Javon's Addiction
- Cause & Effect
- Breaking News
- Flirting With Disaster
- C4
- Seductive Silhouette
- Racism
- Divorce
- The Hole
- Lost Teenager
- The Wrecking
- Chemical Romance
- Stalker III
- W.H.O.
- Little D.
- Heart Of The City
- Frequency
- Happy Valentines Day 16
- Indulgence

- Misery Loves Company
- The Product
- Love And War
- Needle And Thread
- Tune In Love
- Signs
- Fatal Devastation
- Love: In It Or Making It
- Fight
- The Brand
- Veteran's Day
- The Outfit
- Stress Out
- The Return
- Is It Over?
- Love Adversity
- Transformation
- Above & Beyond Love
- Sweet Sable
- Most Wanted
- King Of Hearts
- Short & Sweet
- Reckless: Young & Dumb
- The Jungle
- Current Status
- Fragrance: Poetry
- Kiss
- Reckless: Redemption
- Alcohol Reclamation
- Legacy

Follow the candle light

I got a full schedule ready for tonight

Go to the bathroom where the candles are shinning bright

Where the rose petals are on the floor to set the mood right

I'm glad you accepted my private invite

You provided my mind with powerful in site

I'll aboard your body like an air flight

You can record the video and the sound bites

Of our love making, please no stage fright

You can hold and grab that pillow tight

As me and temptation continues to fight

As I rub you down with oils as I proceed to excite

Your imagination on this very special night

You're laced in a see through gown of all white

As I undress my tasteful delight

I aim to please her and I know what she like

As my hands walk up her body like I'm on a hike

As my tongue ride up her legs like a mountain bike

I receive great benefits and no need for a strike

I can't wait until our bodies unite

As she explodes like a stick of dynamite

She got me feeling higher than a space satellite

I performed good but she stole the spotlight

She was worth the excitement and all the hype

LIFETIME ENGAGEMENT

This moment is sentimental

These words is the voice for this instrumental

This love is real and very confidential

I want to make up the love differential

I love to draw our relationship in pencil

Tracing the words "committed" in stencil

You are a superior woman and very influential

I took this stand today because of your potential

I want to take this to the next level, lets make this official

We need a pastor to make this love traditional

This love we have is true and not fictional

I want to love your heart, soul and body in the physical

To bring you joyful times and never make you miserable

Spending an eternity with you is serious and not critical

This love is wonderful and spiritual

We can be the first to come up with our own love ritual

This proves to you that I love you unconditional

Your my precious jewel and your my miracle

I want our love to be innovative and unpredictable

That's why I love being poetic and lyrical

This announcement will be broadcast live on your stereo

Record this Kodak moment live on video

As we riding in our just married vehicle

I want to make WILL YOU MARRY ME visible

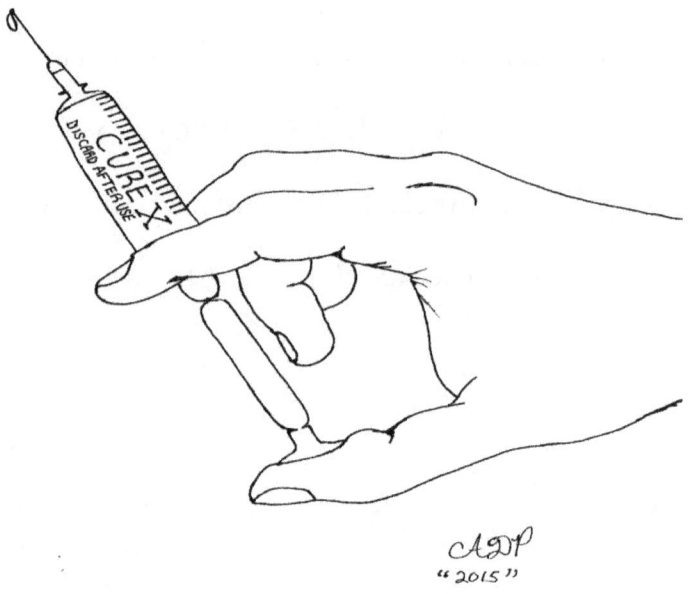

THE CURE

I've been watching your health deteriorate

It's so many different words that can illustrate

This illness, sickness and suffering diseased filled trait

I wish this were a mistake

As we pray to keep you well and awake

Seeing you lying in the bed got to irritate

Your body and soul but how much can it tolerate?

This virus, this affliction as we pray and meditate

We can't let this affection dictate

What we need to get is research to heal and to medicate

To constantly shield you and elevate

The awareness and health rate

Of the people of the United States

And the world and watch it demonstrate

The cure and treatment please let me elaborate

The reason for the words that I collaborate

Is to re ensure possibilities that we activate

Guaranteed to flutter and make your heart shake

The hands of those who participate

In volunteering because we do appreciate

The services to help fight the diseases that intimidate

My goal is to annihilate and make the illnesses disintegrate

When I hug you it feels like the best connection

Like a quarterback throwing his wide receiver a touchdown reception

I caught your love with deep affection

I can see us in the mirror, what a beautiful reflection

I know what is real and this is no deception

I can see love already went in this direction

I want to take your ravishing body and add it to my art collection

That's right after I do my full body inspection

Canvassing every little detail and every section

As your body define the word perfection

Your face has a divine complexion

With the eyes of the best selection

Only God can create this blessing

That is breath taking and refreshing

Let my hands teach your body the lesson

As she begins to start undressing

I massage her mind causing her misdirection

She thought it was going to be nothing but sexing

Because I admit we did a little sexting

On the phone but it was no stressing

I touched her mind with my words falling like precipitation

I grabbed her soul with my verbal communication

She was amused by the words of this conversation

It was worth all the anticipation

Laying her body down on the bed for this evaluation

Full body mechanics used in this situation

As I touched her heart and her body started trembling and shaking

Our eyes are locked at the right location

Our lips met at the perfect destination

My hands on top of your hands when we are facing

Our hearts are singing love songs and it sounds so amazing

How my tongue can give your body a good vibration

I call this love in the making.....

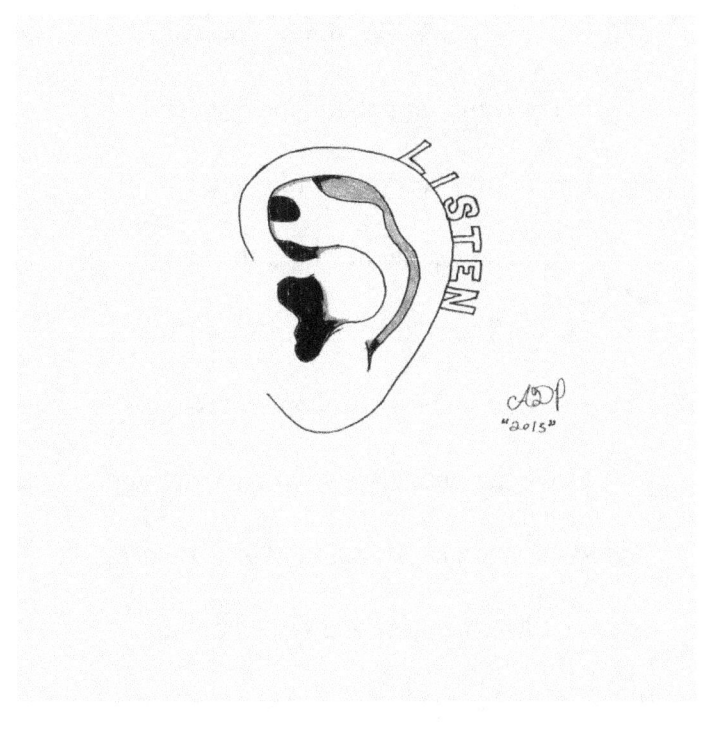

Once again I felt like I lost my friend

I feel like no one understand s the man within

Nobody see the pain, agony, torment but my pen

The suicide rains down my face of sin

The drama that really kills me over and over this is not pretend

This is my cry for help to end this trend

I'm so deep in debt with no money to spend

I'm trying to talk but no one can hear the trouble and anxiety blend

I'm waiting on someone's heart and hands to extend

Their love to me like sunrays on your skin

I'm waiting on that hope dividend

Am I crazy or am I legend

Am I a visionary or am I the lesson

That I keep on stressing

I need you lord, my only blessing

I love her but hell is what I'm catching

I need her and I'm not going to give up begging

I love her kids and I'm pledging

100% honesty, loyalty, love and no disrespecting

Please accept this as a invitation, an apology of this hateful skin I'm shedding

MY PROPOSAL

I know we had our ups and downs

Our great days and worst days

But we made it through the harsh sounds

And we celebrated together many birthdays

It's been a boxing match and we been through 12 rounds

We can watch our life in instant replay

Or run it through an ultrasound

Sorry for the delay

But its time for you to be crowned

With a royal and extravagant display

That will make you smile and you will never frown

This day and everyday

I will show the whole city and town

What I've wrote on this essay

That you are a for sure shot and not a rebound

As you stand tall and shine from the sun ray

Its love, trust and hope that we have found

Now I can call you my fiancé

If you accept this proposal as my knee touches the ground

And I promise if you accept that everything will be okay

RESURRECTION

I was dead, no pulse and no heart beat

I'm laying here lifeless in the street

I was quite, alone and never wanted to speak

I felt like I couldn't walk but had 2 feet

I really couldn't eat

I felt like I was a stone or a piece of concrete

I was frozen and then I felt a little heat

It was her who pulled me out of defeat

This divorce that had made me weak

She made my pain obsolete

She had me on my first winning streak

Without her my life is incomplete

She took my soul beyond mountains and higher peaks

She took me into her private suite

Where she built my confidence and my new physique

She removed the tears that rolled down from my cheek

She transformed me in about a week

Her impact was hitting me like rain or sleet

As I continue to compliment her on this sheet

The words I have for her need no adjustments or tweaks

She is beyond a dime, a 10... man she is elite

She got that love you can't erase or delete

She breathe the air back in me with her new technique

Reviving me back from this temporary sleep

I was counting the days of depression and not sheep

This is my spoken word and she produced the beat.........

I'm Resurrected.....thanks

JAVON'S ADDICTION

I can't shake it off; she got me strung out badly

I'm addicted to her smell, walk, and personality

I feel her syringe running through my veins rapidly

The love oozing inside my soul it feels naturally

This was my addiction

It was a toxic creature of science fiction

She had me looking, searching but I only can see her in my vision

She cuts at my heart with swift precision

The force felt like a head on collision

Her love left me no choices, options or decisions

I tried to cook up her in the kitchen

I realized she is pure and not freebase that's the difference

That puts me in a very tough position

She is my fix for avidity and ambition

She is the only one left untouched in mint condition

She is the only one with a very detailed description

She is the reason why I'm living

I will find her and that is my prediction

I don't care if I'm out of my jurisdiction

When it comes to her I have no restrictions

I need her because she is my daily prescription

The only way you can keep me away from her is death or put me in prison

She is my hope and love's only religion

My belief is strong just like a Christian

No need for disputes or contradictions

You can't replicate her; she is the authentic invention

With a high that leaves me in another dimension

With the side effects of symbolic intentions

I found her phone number but it was missing the extension

I found myself back on this obsessive mission

I give you my all

My love that stands so tall

You got my heart bouncing like a ball

As I wait desperately for your phone call

I'm trying to sit still but now my mind is starting to crawl

Was that my last time speaking to her as my heart begins to fall

I feel trapped between these four walls

And my patience is getting very small

Now her love is fallen down on me like Lake effect snow squalls

I'm trying to find directions to love's shopping mall

But I'm lost because I'm either at the wrong store walking down the wrong hall

I thought I saw her face at the wrong place…. but na'll

My queen will never fool with ya'll

She is the best thing that only GOD can draw

I drink her love by the gallons I don't need no straw

She has no scratches; no dents and she don't have any flaws

When she walks pass me, my heart gives her a round of applause

I just hope that when she finally comes back that she sign love's special clause

Her together and me forever is love's only cause!

They took the prayer out of school

Now the kids of today have no rules

No discipline, no standards they acting like fools

Making babies, being disrespectful and calling each other garden tools

People use to swim peacefully now they are getting shot at the swimming pool

It feels like a car with no fuel

They think going to jail or juvie is being cool

Remember your life is a precious jewel

Respect is earned and you got give it too

You're 12 years old worrying about sex and getting tattoos

You are creating chaos and the next taboos

The devil is eating this up like cashews

Once he unleash the beast it might snatch you

Murder rates up, sinning and repenting is past due

You got these negative thoughts going through your head like shampoo

These streets will hurt you or murder your crew

You try to escape but you stuck like glue

We all dressed in black and your mom needs tissue

Because the pastor is saying things that are not true

No legacy left behind, so what good did you do?

FLIRTING with DISASTER

Rain on me

All on me

Love pouring down slowly

Through my heart, so listen closely

It feels warm and very toasty

This kind of love deserves a plaque or a trophy

That feels nice, soft and cozy

People want to see what it is, they're so noisy

They can see the love flowing through my veins

As I sweat away the hurt and pain

The heart breaks and stress constantly running through my brain

Causing mayhem and disaster like a cyclone or a hurricane

Mass destruction and who is to blame?

While my heart is whipped and beaten and wrapped around these chains

As i lay down in a pool of blood bitten by loves fangs

But its crazy how love is great and then it can change

But did it change? Well lets check the stains

Lets open our eyes and remember the name

Love has the best service with unlimited range

Hate disguises as love and you think its the same

Your love is the quarterback getting sack in this game

Fighting for the win but hate is the winner oh, what a shame

Hate has your heart on its wall hanging in a frame

But love conquers hate no matter the size of its flame

SHATTERED

Picking up the pieces from my heart

I can't believe that it's been ripped apart

Placed on a shelf and thrown in a shopping cart

Your more than a woman, you're a work of art

Its so much to say about you but I don't know where to start

Your like an album that's number one on the billboard charts

I'm just waiting on a little light or just a little spark

But all I got is depression and I'm left in the dark

I'm lost and I got to find some where to park

My love but it has scratches and a bunch of marks

From gun shots, bombs, knives and a bunch of darts

Thrown at me but I got to use my smarts

I'm wounded and left for dead as lay in this tank of sharks

Bleeding as they feeding off my pain and anguish

Sitting in this prison suffering from being hurt and languish

I need to redeem my life and her realms to vanquish

This breakup is deadly and dangerous

Full of tears, nightmares and many changes

If this kills me I wont become rich or famous

I wish this relationship was easy and painless

No matter the damage to this love it remain stainless

I can't believe that love has another door

There is another island across the shore

I never witness something this phenomenal before

The feeling is so demanding I know I need more

The urge is so tempting my mind has hit the floor

I need to find something to kill my appetite for you at the store

But the craving got my heart sore

You got my heart rotten to the core

As I watched my love grow wings like a bird and soar

It's like watching my favorite singer go on tour

Or watching her leave the country to go to war

It's like seeing the rich feeding the poor

It's like seeing your favorite sports player score

Trust me, I need to drift away in your soul and explore

It's something important that you can't ignore

Love is in you, look what it got in store

It's us two divided by 4

Join as one explosive device call us C4

An Explosion of love causing uproar

The impact you can feel it from Cleveland to Singapore

It is you I will love always and adore

Seductive Silhouette

I'm sitting down waiting

Full of anticipation

She got my full participation

She kissing on my neck and she got my heart racing

She got my hormones set for detonation

As she sits on my lap, I guess it's time for some roll playing

You can be my secret agent of an investigation

I'm handcuffed no need for emancipation

We can do whatever you want it's no limitations

I watched her hands heal my body like medication

This is our way to release frustration

As we put together our own photo publication

Or a late night show on a T.V. station

I give you my attention and my full dedication

What we are doing is redefining the word gravitation

As our bodies and minds are in full meditation

As we intertwine body directions and rotations

It feels like this love in the making

This way beyond any temptation

This is love's new classification

Racism

Don't we all have 2 lungs?

Two kidneys

Two hands

Two legs

Two feet

Two eyes

Two ears

We have been enslaved for over 400 years

We speak the same language, so what do you fear?

Through all the hostility and hate we're still here

Why do you act that way is very unclear?

We all don't wear sagging pants and drink 40 ounces of beer

It's because of a dream that has brought us here

Living equal in America is what we want to persevere

But for some reason they use enmity and antipathy to interfere

With our goals and vision that is pure

My skin should not be a spear

That cuts deeply in my soul

As they kept my heart as a souvenir

I'm adding up the suffering and malaise like a cashier

They're subtracting the merriment, hilarity, buoyancy and cheer

This is beyond a job and beyond a career

Beyond money, beyond basketball and beyond this hemisphere

This is like a terrorist attack that is severe

I want the hate, envy and racism to disappear

I know it's hard as a child to deal with change

I know how life can really feel strange

Your parents have split apart but it's hard to explain

To some people it might make the kids go deranged

They watch their parents call each other out of their names

Observing arguments that lead to chaos like broken picture frames

The kids watching the marriage burst into flames

These altercations lead to police sirens with no fun and games

Which parent will feel ashamed?

But neither parent was using their brain

As they watched the rain

Roll down the Windowpane

As the madness leaves a stain

The sadness is hard to contain

As the children go through the pain

It's not your fault mom and dad lifestyle is rearranged

I know it feels like hate is being exchanged

The negativity is stuck to your brain

Please don't feel like you're the one to blame

I find myself back in this hole

But loving you is all I know

I want to fall upon your heart like snow

but I'm laying here dying talking to the black crow

I want to live so I can really show

You that love is real and see how far it will go

I feel like I failed you and I'm at my all time low

I can't understand why I can't earn your soul

But loving you is my ultimate goal

I want to attach my love on your flagpole

But I can't because I'm back in this hole

I'm burning up like a piece of charcoal

I want to serve you all my love in a hot bowl

That's been boiling on top of my stove

But I can't because I keep falling in this hole

I keep fighting but now it's taking a toll

Engineering a painful death blow by blow

I can see it happening as time is moving very slow

I just want to give you my love in a box wrapped up with a bow

Unravel the gift and because my heart has fallen to the floor

I'm begging for more and more

Of your love that I can't ignore

That I lost all my riches in love and now I'm poor

I'm losing you and I want to tie the score

But all I see is my heart floating across the seashore

Pulling me back in this hole like tug of war

I need your love to make me soar

Out of this pit for sure

I'm not rotten please check out my core

I'm aching and I'm feeling kind of sore

I want to go back on tour

To show you that I do adore

Everything that you have in store

Please give me a chance that's me knocking on the door

I'm singing the melody by Stevie Wonder "My Cherie Amour"

With roses and I got plenty of more

Love coming and I got two glasses to pour

Do you accept my invitation to finally explore?

I'm soak in pity and I don't know where to go.....

LOST TEENAGER

You're smoking, you're fighting, you're drinking, you're cussing,

You're sexing, you're hustling, you're struggling, you're angry,

You're sad, you're mad, you're full of hate, you're hopeless,

You're not focused, you're uneducated, you're frustrated,

You're lazy, you're crazy, you're disrespectful, you're not intellectual,

You're negative, you're cancer, you're evil, you're sinister,

You're young, you're going to change, you're great,

You're amazing, you're a child of God, you're phenomenal,

You're unstoppable, you're that light, you're beautiful,

You're unique, you're innovative, you're humble, you're human,

You're very special, you're the best, you're real, you're enlightened,

You're a boss but without God you will stay LOST!

Is sex better than love?

Why do people prefer pigeons over doves?

Why do we like to be pushed or shoved?

Why we cant we touch love without a glove?

Its hard to keep your head above

The water when you are standing in a puddle full of

Hate that is holding a loaded gun up to your heart

You're watching the instant reply of your heart being ripped apart

Piece by piece by this menacing beast

Controlled by this two legged freak

With no love, no hope and no peace

Just your mind and heart at the dinner table as it begins to feast

It needs you to be deceased

Pumping hate through it veins as the rate of hate increased

It's biting you daily with all of its teeth

You must escape its claws of disbelief

But don't be found underneath its feet

To be stomp on laying lifeless on the concrete

This animal has no heart beat

He just has your heart beat

He chews your heart up like a piece of meat

It's so devastating for you to speak

Because your feelings and emotions have you weak

It sees you as the trick and the treat

Controlling your life without you saying a peep

It looks at you as a sheep

And you look at him as a white sheet

Or a nightmare on Elm Street

The drama is so deep

It hunts you in your sleep

Everybody is enjoying the show from their front row seat

People get to witness your soul in defeat

But now is the time for you to meet

Confidence, motivation and courage at its highest peak

If it's off balance we can adjust the volume or make a few tweaks

Stay positive and believe in yourself all the time not just a few weeks

Stay humble and genuine and keep your business out the streets

Chemical Romance

She is truly irresistible

She is captivating and invincible

Her love is futuristic like it's in digital

Rhythmic words like it's a musical

Her sexiness is clearly visible

These are not punch lines this is all lyrical

I love her mentally and also physical

I never been through something this critical

She is ravishing, desirable and my miracle

Her touch feels inspiring and very spiritual

She is royalty and she is the imperial

Our romance contains love potions mix with that love chemical

THE STALKER

III

I'm walking to my car

I heard a voice from a far

All of a sudden I see a man with a scar

With a gun and his breathe smell like he was at a bar

He had a ski mask on and he was smoking a cigar

I'm staring at the barrel of his gun and man this is bizarre

Give me your money, phone and jewelry he shouted out loud

Not a witness in site and I was praying for a crowd

No cameras, no police not even a single cloud

Of joy but evil was the only thing allowed

He cocked back his gun and now he feels proud

I told him please don't shoot me I won't tell

He said shut up; I'm going to send straight to hell

Toe tag in a body bag is where your body will dwell

You bet not scream or yell

I'm not going back inside that jail cell

I'm not asking for bail

This will not be my last tale

I got a child starving and my wife isn't doing well

I got to come back with something I cannot fail

My heart will show you my lifetime trail

Lift your chin up, as my chest began to inhale then exhale

I closed my eyes wishing this were a fairytale

My body temperature is hotter than a summer in Fort Lauderdale

He grabs my shirt near my throat, now I'm turning pale

I heard a voice saying "welcome Javon to my pay scale"

This is death pay attention to the details

I've seen bodies lying with the seashells

I sent you death threats through many emails

You thought you escaped my fury

I replied, I see things more clearly

I got to live my life more purely

I got to make better choices and decisions

I got to use better knowledge and wisdom

I felt someone grab my shoulder

And I stood up on my feet

Just realizing my daughter woke me up out of my

Sleep.....(Wooooooooooooooooo whipping my forehead)

W.H.O.

W.H.O.? , World health organization

To increase the health of this earthly location

Plastic bottles, paper, cardboard please recycle we need your participation

Boosting eco life is the topic and situation

Unhealthy car and truck smoke causing air pollution

We need to pick up litter off the ground let's start an evolution

Let's make our community clean and spotless and let's stop abusing

Drug needles and crack pipes I got plastic or recycle bins which are you choosing?

We need soil, dirt and water for the plants we growing what are you using?

LITTLE D.

D. is surrounded by bed bugs and roaches

His sibling's faces are full of drool and mucus running from their noses

House full of trash and rats running through the sofas

Posted on the door is a 30-day notice

They don't eat healthy; all they drink is Kool Aid and sodas

The parents on drugs and they can't get the addiction of their shoulders

They high off heroine, crack and they are chain smokers

D has no clothing, no food and no focus

D got to boil water to bathe and he's feeling hopeless

D is waking up to gunshots, fire trucks, police and not a hot cup of Folgers

D's father is on America's Most Wanted crime posters

The neighborhood is full of boarded houses and foreclosures

D is living the life of helicopters and TV. Reporters

What's crazy there is no law and order?

D's patience is getting shorter and shorter

It feels like he has 3 seconds left in the 4th quarter

In a game that he is losing that feels like torture

He can't read because illiteracy has a grip on his culture

He's among nothing but crabs in the barrel and vultures

This is someone's family treasure

Now they are dealing with strokes and high blood pressure

Tremendous amounts of stress no one could ever measure

This heart disease is full of rainy days and bad weather

It's not only your fight it's ours we can do this together

I'm installing hope, love, confidence and motivation in this letter

This is one of many ways for your health to get better

This time we are going to be the aggressor

As God teach us remedies and lessons like a professor

We can call our community the investor

They donate time, income and do whatsoever

We must consistently endeavor

If we are to succeed to beat this dreadful sector

I see your tears and pain like spots on a leopard

We can start exercising and dieting just to make an effort

Quit smoking, get organized and end this terror

I see you going through excruciating pain lying on that stretcher

I'm doing my best to balance this life's ledger

I'm producing you a new heart call me the director

A soul full of optimism and aspirations that is stellar

The heart of the city is going up top as my header

I'm working on me

So people can say we

Let love be

The topic and the key

To make the word more frequently

Broadcasted only on this frequency

As it swim in the sea of tranquility

As it increase the chances of my probability

It's so pliable with its versatility

With great amounts of agility

As it practice and compete in this facility

If it weren't for love this wouldn't be a possibility

The kind of love the will murder negativity

We celebrate with these lines

To let you know love is not blind

To represent all mankind

And to hold up my love sign

Like we marching in a picket line

The kind of love that fits my design

With these words that rhyme

This way and all the time

You deserve a monument or a golden shrine

I'm glad I have you in your prime

This is a chance to rewind

The highlights of cards candy and wine

No matter how dark it is you continue to shine

I just want to wish you a Happy Valentines

Indulgence

I've been through a lot of hating

Arguments and plenty of debating

People always saying something about my situation

Sitting down critiquing and evaluating

They know the problem but they can't figure the equation

Of me and her conversation

Which is the new form of communication

Through love, in which is our association

In our hearts is the place and location

Full of passion that keep our hearts racing

It separates love from lust and love from infatuation

And we both relieve our frustration

Through intimate clouds of precipitation

Affectionate principles of relaxation

As I entered the warmness of her private foundation

A place where I love to visit often and vacation

Which I went beyond her imagination

It was a lot of talking, buckling and shaking

It was perfect, the best collaboration

It was the introduction of physical education

It has no limit and no expiration

Because we both got the qualifications

That makes love real and not an imitation

I can put it in words but I will give you my poetic illustration

What we got is like a corporation

Partners for life there will be no liquidation

Just the words "I LOVE YOU" in quotation

Misery Loves Company

Drunken in her night of fun

As her husband heart continues to run

Away from the vows and together as one

He waits to see her face but all he see is the sun

No phone call, no communication, there was none

Walking through the door breath of liquor and vomiting, yep she is done

Kids asleep asking where is mom at and I called her a quarter past one

No answer and thoughts begin in my head

Is she cheating? Or is she dead?

I'm cussing and mad and full of dread

This is the second time she has done this, as my face turns red

I want this to work but she hasn't care what I have said

As the anger of my soul continues to spread

I know I'm not perfect but I'm working and bring home the bread

She chooses to go out on school nights instead

Walking back home in the middle of the night, that's not using your head

I try to go to sleep but I keep tossing and turning in my bed

She tells me Ill be home in a soon

Hours past and ANGER is what she fed!

The Product

All I see is drugs

No love, no kisses and no hugs

A lot of Drug dealers, child molesters, killers and thugs

Housing with ants, roaches, rats and bed bugs

Beer bottles, needles, litter and gun slugs

There is nothing but fear, negativity and evil filled in these jugs

Spilled over by city officials as they drink coffee in their mugs

No life to your apartment complex because you pulled the plug

A place full of anger, gossip, drama, karma and bad blood

Causing drastic destruction like an avalanche or like a flash flood

Why did you throw her brand new clothes in the mud?

But she caught you naked with another female in the bathtub

I know she need to stop drinking and always going to the club

I know what's missing in you all, where's the LOVE?

All you want to do is cuss, fight and push and shove

All you need to do is calm down and leave it to the man above

He will set you free like a dove

Is this how it feels when its over with?

You took my heart and drunk it up like a fifth

I thought feeling past the bottom was a lie or a myth

I can't go to sleep like I'm working third shift

It attack me hard, quick and swift

This heartbreak is a curse not a gift

It felt like love threw my a$$ off a cliff

But I didn't die as I lay down unconscious and stiff

Laying here buried in this snowdrift

I'm lost on this road of depression and I need a lift

As the misery hit me like bullets made by a Gunsmith

I can't breathe, I can't eat, and I can't speak

I feel very sluggish and weak

As I look at my mind drifting across a creek

And my soul dropped past my feet

As love chewed on it like a piece of meat

I found out the true meaning of defeat

All I hear is the words to this song but no heartbeat

It continues to break and the blood begins to leak

My heart feels empty and very incomplete

Non-important and obsolete

I wish I could take this back but love has no receipt

In love and war you got to know when to retreat

I keep living this episode like its on repeat

I'm tired of reading this torment on a spreadsheet

Only God can mend a broken heart and push delete

On all the problems that will leave you bittersweet

needle & thread

I'm sorry for all I done

I love you because you're my number one

You shine brighter than the sun

If this love can be weighed, its way pass a ton

I thank you for all the great times and unlimited fun

I don't want you to run

I need you like bullets need a gun

Or like a hamburger need a bun

I'm trying to add up this sum

But I was the one who was that bum

That unearthly scum

That bad piece of chewing gum

I deserve to get beat like a drum

As I drank your heart away like some rum

I feel very stupid and dumb

You should have a whole slice of love and not a crumb

I'm sorry for what I have become

I should have follow the rule of thumb

But I live like I was in the slum

I want to go back to where I won

Your heart and now I'm stun

Please accept my tears of apology from

Love and this is my last song

Forgive me and I will give up my other lung

I apologize for all the chaos and hurt in this song ....

This love is so amazing

Your heart I keep on chasing

A love that is incredible, hot and blazing

You got my temperature high and you got my heart racing

When it comes to your beauty it will be no replacing

No matter what people say about us let them keep on hating

They are not like you because you're Gods best creation

I want the world to know you're my queen across the country and the nation

As we ride in love and your heart is my destination

To touch your heart in so many ways with censure deep penetration

You have been on my mind since yesterday distracting all my concentration

This is my soundtrack to your heart that love compilation

I'm going start my own group my own love organization

Put your hand on my heart and tell me do you feel the love vibration

You're my cup of coffee for the morning, my strength and my motivation

A love like this deserves an award with a standing ovation

While you tune in live to my love radio station!

I can't believe that this is real

It feels like I signed a multi billion-dollar deal

Only if you knew how I feel

This love is delivered to you signed and sealed

With my heart and it's been a big thrill

I've climbed over every mountain and travel over these hills

To see your face when you swallow this pill

Called love and I revealed

This love that's hard as a rock and shining like steel

When I see you girl I got to kneel

You're not a snack; you're a full coarse meal

I know your heart is still bleeding and it need time to heal

Here is the key to my heart and now you can steer the wheel

I'm walking around the mind of confusion

I found a problem and now I'm sitting

On hope and I'm tired from running from these tragedies

I'm dealing with Satan

I'm facing racist people who are constantly hating

I'm still stuck in this membrane

I'm shaking and trembling

I think I'm going insane

Maybe I'm psychotic and bizarre

I'm soaked in gasoline looking deranged

I need a match to start this heated exchange

The fury runs through my eyes of hysteria

I've been fighting crime in bloodstains

I feel ruthless and sadistic

That's why they have me in shackles and chains

This is making me crazy and ballistic

Am I the contestant or the critic?

I seen vengeance in all shades of her lipstick

The adrenaline possessed my abilities to see beyond my sight

I need to end this tension and this urge to deliver my wrath

I need to feed this wild animal and end this appetite

Of destruction and of mayhem

These are the scars of my skin

Tattooed on my body and soul

They show that I'm guilty as sin

Living in another world you can't imagine

The door is open in my mind

Are you sure you want to come in?

LOVE: IN IT OR MAKING IT

This is amazing

Love that we just keep on chasing

You keep love hot and blazing

Your love is for anytime or any occasion

You're love's topic of the day and top conversation

Do you feel how hard love hit from the ground shaking?

From my heart that big love vibration

Anything other than you is a true imitation

You are God's greatest creation

All i got is my love and I want to make a donation

To your heart which is my favorite location

I'll take you in my care for further observation

I want to welcome you to my association

Full of fantasies and great imagination

I need your full attention and participation

It will be a lot of lovemaking and straight penetration

I will hand cuff you for this investigation

No hands needed to give this evaluation

All I need is opportunity and hard concentration

I hope your body is ready for this preparation

Because my hands don't have a particular stop or destination

Both of our souls connected for the greatest collaboration

It's all love and I'm not in desperation

I learned from love, now I'm ready for graduation

Thanks for your time and your cooperation

They attack your mind like killer bees

As I marinate energy over these ABC's

Telling me how poetry supposed to be

But you can't tell me how to be me

You can't jail my thoughts because I'm free

I don't have to pay my publisher a fee

Because of my team, I do things independently

Self motivated and it's very spiritually

I need to touch your soul individually

One by one it's feel so effortlessly

The devil tries to break me down mentally

But it's one rule we can live by just simply

By believing you can have a Rolls Royce or a Bentley

Whatever makes your life happy

But I will never be a victim or a casualty

Of things that cause negativity

Or live in somebody else's misery

Or harm myself physically

Or make myself sickly

Or be ungrateful or picky

I'll never stand still I'm very shifty

I only can get it done by being so risky

I use my achievements for my publicity

Are you with me? Or are you against me?

If you for me, use this motivation and drink it like whiskey

If you drink too much you won't be leveled but tipsy

Clear your mind from the thoughts that are filthy

Live life purely and you won't feel guilty

THE BRAND

Look in the mirror

Things have not been any clearer

You don't have to dream small, imagine bigger

Don't under estimate yourself just make a larger figure

Keep focus and don't be a motivation killer

Get your life together and stop being a stripper

I'm not judging you and I want to see you sparkle like glitter

Go get your goals together and don't be a quitter

Build your confidence by reading this scripture

You got the image for the perfect picture

You got so much potential; you are the pick of the litter

Don't be the cause of your own death by pulling the trigger

Don't let negative thoughts cut your faith like a pair scissors

Do all the right things to make you the ultimate victor

Do the things to uplift your soul to make you wealthy or be richer

Be that true friend, aunt, mother and sister

Use your passion, vision and determination to make you a winner

<u>Veteran's Day</u>

Thank you for making me a writer and a reader

You're sharing my dreams right now and you created a believer

Keep this as an token of success and not an under achiever

A veteran who can write to you or hear my voice through your speaker

I'm bottle up like a soda you can sell me by the liter

I keep my stuff hot, plug me up like I'm a heater

I write from the heart and you can never call me a cheater

I'm the cook and you can consider yourself an eater

This is my friend and I know how to treat her

I won't let these publishers, authors, and agents beat her

They want to park near her like she's a meter

They want to build a dam around her like a beaver

They want to get in her clothes which is my lines and my style which is her sneakers

Standing in the door way as imposters faking as greeters

Beautiful blue skies

All I see is love in those pretty brown eyes

Words of encouragement from those juicy delicious lips

She's the work of God from head to toe and the way she shift those hips

Her smile can express a billion words

She's known around world, the hood, and suburbs

Known for achieving and succeeding

She's not about fake nails and hair weaving

She's a woman I can believe in

When I need her help when I'm taking a beating

She can heal these wounds and stop the bleeding

What I got here is a woman with love in her heart and soul no need for repeating

STRESS OUT

How can I build my house when you keep borrowing wood and bricks?

How can I do magic if you already know my tricks?

Why every time I buy something you look at me sick?

Like you can't get a job are too lazy to get welfare or WIC?

But you use my gas, my belongings, and my electric

You watch my TV's and sleep on my couch you give me a headache

I'm taking care of my own family I can't get no credit

It's driving my crazy I don't run off gas that's unleaded

I finally spoke up and said it

If you didn't hear it hopefully you probably read it

This is straight to the meat not something that was breaded

Nothing Fried, season, or shredded

I love you but you don't know what direction I'm headed

I feel like my mind is drying out from all the times I have sweated

My heart is not a rest until you let it

THE RETURN

I've been lost and lonely for a while

I was so beaten I just threw in the white towel

Because I thought it was all over

Just because I didn't see you over my shoulder

I couldn't go another round

Then I got hit with this blow and love came falling down

All I had left was lying on the ground

All you heard was a boom followed by a rumbling sound

And my heart will **pound** and **pound**

It was either swim to shore or stay under and drown

I was out for the count

So much love lost I couldn't even add up the amount

I had went to rehab to recover

From our separation which made me a better lover

A better man with a working plan

Thanks to God and his mercy I'm doing all I can

Love has taught and I have learn

He has brought me back for this possible **Return**

IS IT OVER?

It breaks my soul

To see a crush plan or an injured goal

Or a damaged dream

With no shoulder for you to lean

When you're sad or you need to blow some steam

Each tear represents a struggle or a problem

Looking to God just knowing he can solve them

It's all pain, stress, and shame

You feel like it's all your fought because you have no one else to blame

Thinking to yourself how last year left and came

It feels like your life is on pause and it's not a game

Still feel shackle up with this mental chain

Waiting for the sun to shine so it can end this hurtful rain

LOVE ADVERSITY

Stop all this madness!

End all this sadness!

I wish I had this

Love, but all I got is my status

My ego might had been the fattest

But with you in my life you always make me the gladdest

Man, with my heart beating the fastest

You made me a savage

Of love we are like corn beef and cabbage

With a love above average

Shinning like 16 karats

Which equals a loving marriage

We got two horses pulling love inside this carriage

Love did me a favor

Showed me the colors of being a life saver

Being somebody's inspiration and motivator

Created a love maker

Not a baby maker

If I can't have this love they might as well place with an undertaker

Better known as a heartbreaker

Shaking my heart like a salt shaker

Please I promise to remain your lover and not a hater...

Transformation

I can see beyond what I've been seeing

Sadness was just a way of being

I found out the true meaning

Of nothing, but that's why I'm freeing

The past from my way of speaking

It's something that was revealed in one weekend

I am the beholder except for when internally sleeping

Open your eyes and let yourself do the teaching

Manifesting and preaching

Do allot more of loving and reaching

Out to others

Not just to your sisters and brothers

Cousins, uncles, aunts, fathers, and mothers

Grow relationships to form friends and something other...

Above & Beyond Love

Love conquers all evil

Love is what we need to survive as people

Love is what makes all marriages equal

Love makes a bad relationship a happy sequel

Love is stopping me from retaliating

Love isn't spreading rumors about me so why are you participating?

Love is God so why you acting like Satan?

Love isn't war, fighting, or debating

Love is unity, trust, and communicating

Love isn't lust, porn, or fornicating

Love is something lovers keep creating

Love isn't something you should be saturating

Love is patient and always in the making

Love can leave you in suspense and have your heart shaking

Love is protection from your heart breaking

Love has it's own identity there will be no mistaking

Love is always in your face but you're always steady chasing

Love away with constant dating and replacing

Love is a question that many people will be facing

Love is the answer for many relationships that are aging

Love is the reason that many hearts are inflating

Love is the right reason why we are celebrating

Sweet Sable

Go and prepare dinner at the table

Dim the lights and turn off the cable

Turn on the music if you're able

And get her prepared for the poem sweet sable

And undress her from the chest down to her navel

She is brown like the syrup of maple

She got my tongue stuck to her body like a staple

She don't have to worry about me not being faithful

Long as she make me feel grateful

I like her; she's very playful

4 ways to four play from January to April

I won't stop unless she says so

Her body is soft like play doe

I formed the shape of someone who is special

She had more moves than somebody who wrestles

She got my blood rushing through my vessels

All you hear is love shots and missiles

And my harmonies shooting like pistols

And after we finish I'm going to miss those

Rookie moments and how we became pros

How we got to this point nobody knows

About us and these Sweet Sables

This is a story

About a woman's glory

About a woman's pain

It left a few spots and a little stain

A smart woman with so much to gain

Flying over relationships like an airplane

It's not her fault but she takes all the blame

Sick of how men left and came

One out the door and things are still the same

She's all screwed up with a lot of shame

She wants to go right but she's stuck in the same lane

Made a wrong turn and its time for a change

Trying to shoot love but she was out of range

She had four clips of forgiveness and a target with no name

That's what happens when you're dealing with love it's so strange

KING OF HEARTS

Your mind is telling you no but your heart is saying yes

So go over there and end all this stress

Put on your best suit or your best dress

Pick up a gift to show them love is not a test

But to show them you are at your best

Start off with I love you and love will do the rest

Spice up their heart with the words of love expressed

And hope it moves them like a piece from chess

And jump into their arms to clean up the mess

Of anger and hate that was left attached to the flesh

It's break ups to make ups

It's hey what's to say what's

But it's you and them in this shake up

Don't spend too much hate but love is what you want to save up

Quit spending and pretending

Because it's each other's love that you both keep on bending

SHORT & SWEET

My life is empty without you in it

If you must know my love has no limit

This is no pretending, fantasy or gimmick

You are the first and only the rest try to mimic

You can't run out of my love because my warranty is extended

Please forgive me for the things I said wrong don't be offended

When I say I love you always, I meant it!

I will never leave your heart alone or unattended

To hold you, adore you and appreciate you that's what love recommended

I was running from hate but love handcuff me and had me apprehended

You're my judge and my case has been suspended

I'm in your prison where love is 24/7 and misery has ended

I love you and I hope you love that you've been complimented

I'm only 19 years old

I got a good woman at home but my heart is too cold

She cooks and cleans but my ego is to bold

I got like 5 women on the side matter a fact two live down the road

The other three women got the same zip code

One of them makes money off that pole

But sleeping with them was just my only goal

I like the one that can sing like Keisha Cole

I might have to hold on to her like En Vogue

The way she kisses me I'm ready to explode

She got my circuits in overload

My other girl is international across the globe

But I still disrespect the one that treat me like gold

I had to see my other chick in her silky bathrobe

My girlfriend found out and it was murder she wrote

She motioned her finger across her throat

It got to the point I hung myself with some rope

It got tighter as I begin to choke

I was just trying to find the next woman I can poke

I was addicted to sex like a drug fiend to dope

I was reckless to my lady and I lost all hope

My every move was under a microscope

All I do now is eat, drink, have sex and smoke

Now my girlfriend left me starving, lonely and broke

She left me a one-page note

That had various instructions and many quotes

I couldn't go to sleep for days it kept me woke

I blew the best thing I had now I'm looking for an antidote

But all I got was my heart placed in an envelope

This situation was predicted last year in my horoscope

Being a player got my true love revoked

I lost everything and it was her that I should have promote

I didn't give her my time or even my vote

Now I desperately need love to be my coach

Or hit the rewind button on life's remote

I think I need rehab because it's hard to cope

It struck my body like a lighting bolt

Every time I look at our pictures and gifts in my tote

I should have took our relationship seriously and not a joke

Welcome 2 The Jungle

This is the hardest thing in life I had face

I know you have anger that makes your heart race

I know you have that animosity that has a bad taste

As I look in your eyes standing face to face

I look into your heart, which is not in the right place

It has sunken into your pain tied up like a shoelace

I could never cross you and your love is what I need to embrace

It's the greatness and amazement that I love to chase

I wish you could climb the ladder that leads to my heart

I wish I could put the right pieces I need in loves shopping cart

I wish God could tell you how much I really love and appreciate your art

I wish you knew I'm bleeding and watching my heart being ripped apart

I need your heart, love and understanding just a little spark

I need your light to shine on me as I sit in the dark

I need a place in your heart for me to park

My vehicle of love that is so sincere I wish you could see the chart

I wish you knew I never cheated on you

I want the sun and no skies of gray and blue

I need you to know that my love is true

I couldn't just sit back and hurt you

I really do deserve you

I'm willing to die

I'm willing to pay

I'm will to say

My love is real

My heart is broken into pieces of steal

I know you are very hurt and I promise to keep it real

For here on no matter what the deal

I'm sorry that I continue to spill

Negativity on our relationship

I really want to grow and develop love constantly

I'm lost without you

I really need you back in my life

I really, really need you to be my wife

As soon as I get things together

I'm fighting through all this bad weather

I'm hoping you see that things we're getting better

I present to you my love letter

And I promise to never hurt you but to love you forever.

Please accept me back in your heart, I'm crying and I'm dying spiritually

I need you and only you and no one else I promise to put love back on our shelf

Please I pray for forgiveness

But I'm not a villain

I'm not a cheater

I'm a motivator

I'm your soul mate

So please don't hesitate to let your heart see the real me the truth is deeply

Chained with love and care

I promise to never let this love disappear

Hold me, touch me and please feel me

I know I can be the greatest man you ever had

Please let me.....

CURRENT STATUS:
standing on a line between giving up and seeing how much more I can take.

I got the test results back

It sent me in a panic attack

My daughter has cancer and how can I tell her that?

I cried and cried until my eyes turned black

She's so young and nobody expected that

She would be sick and that's a fact

I'm going to do whatever I can because our odds are stacked

Against us but we will not over react

But pray to God to keep us on track

For a healing and to keep her alive and intact

She is suffering from the pain in her lower back

I see the agony in her eyes like her heart was being cracked

By a sledgehammer or constantly being smacked

I'm thinking hard as we driving around in my grandfather's Cadillac

She had big dreams that have been hacked

I've been flying around the country for guidance like I'm a bat

My wings help me add time to her life and subtract

Her sickness and handicap

To rescue her soul out of this trap

God led me to a place on this map

He provided a gift for her to unwrap

As we watched everybody stand up and clap

As promised we had bridged the healing gap

Only these women were chosen

To wear this poetic potion

To stick to your body like lotion

It will definitely have you floating

Like you're standing in an ocean

In a fragrance poetically soaking

If the scent leaves all you have to do is reopen

Something that is soft and spoken

Let me interest you in my deepest pleasures

As I sprinkle my fingertips on your body like pepper

As I massage your body then apply the pressure

As I head south to find her secret treasure

Her body was soft as a feather

Just sit back and let me be the aggressor

Just say what you need me to do because I'll do whatever

In this movie call me the producer and director

Just close your eyes and I'll make it better

Let my love rain on you like stormy weather

We can do this twice a day just call it a double header

This is that new love you can call me trendsetter

We started earlier kissing in the elevator

It's so intense we went from the nightstand to the dresser

I got your heart and soul in my hand and I'll be your protector

Please be my student and I'll be your professor

I'll introduce Kamasutra and 4 play in this lecture

This lovemaking is more than a semester

I want to make it last forever

I'll give you all my love and nothing lesser

As we join hands and lock bodies in this sector

The taste is sweeter than nectar

I'll give her a sign or a gesture

As I showed her how to measure

My love written on this ledger

She got my heart beeping like a smoke detector

If you have any pain afterwards I can make it better

REDEMPTION

My heart was outlined on the ground in chalk

I never experienced this feeling before I could barely walk

I called her phone for months and she didn't want to talk

My immaturity and foolishness finally stopped

As time past I finally stop watching the clock

I worked very hard to finally buy her this rock

But she still had all my phone calls block

I'm trying to put her heart on lock

But I found out that her heart is out of stock

I was confused and very shocked

I wanted to clean my soul but I don't have a bucket or a mop

Now I know how it feels to be on top

And how it feels when somebody has taken your spot

I'm looking up at the stars to connect the dots

She got that outer space love and I can be her astronaut

A wish and a prayer is all I got

I've walked through hell and I will never stop

Fighting for her love until I've bled my last drop

In my body as my heart continues to rot

I Think I'm dying outside in this parking lot

Because my soul is tied up in a knot

And I can't believe I can't escape this awful plot

The feeling was explosive like a gunshot

POW I'm dead!

ALCOHOL RECLAMATION

I notice your heavy drinking

I see your ship slowly sinking

I wrote this letter because I've been thinking

About what you have become and your time is now shrinking

I've seen you laying in your own vomit looking shameful and stinking

Be careful driving or you will see them lights flashing and blinking

Handcuffed and sent to jail sitting with your inner demon

Full of guilt, depression, distress and your mind is constantly screaming

I know you really want an alcohol feeding

To stop the pain and mental bleeding

Your family hopes you stop the horrific consumptions and scheming

Unsteadiness, throwing up and peeing

On yourself is destroying your well being

I know it takes hope, love and passion to give your life a true meaning

I know life has hardships, situations and obstacles that causes weeping

While intoxicated, you're violent and your words are slurred when speaking

Even if you don't hit your loved ones they are still taking a mental beating

Lets get past the fact that you lost your job and you got caught cheating

Now you are stuck in this place having these meetings

In a room for 8 hours destroying your weekends

Your blood alcohol content was over the limit that's why you were speeding

Now you are a student and the law will be doing the teaching

Saying sorry to the kids mother & father crying and pleading

Their child won't have any more birthdays, Christmas or no trick or treating

Lets figure out your mission and new reason

To live better and to survive the whole season

We will get rid of Jack Daniels, Don Julio and St. Pauley's Girl this evening

I know you tired of different people preaching

But it's about defeating and deleting

The temptation of evil that you were eating

Promise to stay committed and never get caught sneaking

A taste of liquor that will stop you from achieving

Your goals and everything you have earned will be depleting

Just work hard and keep on reaching

But if you feel like giving up remember it's not worth leaving

LEGACY

I pledge to love you for eternity

I take an oath to be your security

I promise to never cause you misery

But to give you my love as a special delivery

This moment will go down in history

Not as a myth or a mystery

Holding you high as we triumph in victory

Love can sometimes be slippery

Causing deception and trickery

And large amounts of obscurity

The important part is to maintain our purity

No hate should outlast our durability

Because we used love to build this facility

That's why we maintain stability

Keeping love forever is a great responsibility

It moves with spurts of agility

It stands tall like the Statue of Liberty

Do you know what can kill love? Insecurity

That's why we need to increase the probability

Of faith and positivity

To reach the next level of intensity

To elevate your love physically and mentally

We changed loves identity

And we relocate it to a new embassy

That shows my deepest pleasures and empathy

Full of emotional chemistry

You can't find any similarity

Not even if you are a celebrity

I guarantee only I can do this professionally

It's not based on views or popularity

It's about these words of integrity

Put together on a page so cleverly

This is what we call love therapy

These are the ingredients for this recipe

Now it's finished and you can have a piece of my legacy

www.ingramcontent.com/pod-product-compliance
Lightning Source LLC
Chambersburg PA
CBHW070303230426
43664CB00014B/2622